My Child: 0 to 2 yea.

This book has been published by the HSE (2018). This is the sixth edition (2021). All new parents will be given a copy by your public health nurse when they make their first visit to your home after your baby is born.

'My Child: 0 to 2 years' is filled with expert advice from health professionals in the HSE; like doctors, nurses, psychologists, parenting experts, dietitians and many more.

Our team has worked to give you the best advice on caring for your baby and child. We hope that you can use this book, and our mychild.ie website, as a companion for every step of your child's first early years.

For more information on pregnancy and child health, visit mychild.ie

This is the fifth edition. It was first published in 2005 and last reviewed in 2018.

© Health Service Executive 2018

First published: 2005 (version 1.0)
Reviewed: 2009 and 2018 (version 4.0)
Updated: 2015, 2019, 2020 and 2021 (version 6.0)

This 2021 edition (version 6.0) has updated information on:

- night feeds (page 35)
- formula feeding (page 54)
- vitamin D supplements for your child (pages 56 and 69)
- healthy eating and the children's food pyramid (pages 68 to 72)
- sleeping (pages 73 to 81)
- chickenpox - treatment (page 118)
- child safety - button batteries (pages 181, 192 and 193)
- childcare schemes website address (page 212)

Updates are made to individual sections from time to time. For example, when we become aware of changes to health guidelines or as a result of user feedback.

Reviews take place every few years when the entire book is reviewed by experts.

Your public health nurse: _____

Your health centre: _____

Contents

ISBN: 978-1-78602-111-3

Welcome to My Child: 0 to 2 years

Expert advice for every step

This book provides expert advice from the HSE on baby and toddler health. It is part of a series of books and a website full of information to help you to care for yourself in pregnancy and all through your child's first 5 years.

We asked parents what information would help them most during their child's early years.

Parents told us that they wanted:

- common sense information and tips on the general care of their child
- information about their child's development
- advice about what to do if their child has a problem
- details of the people and services to get in touch with for more help and support

They also told us they wanted this information to be available online and in a printed version to keep at home.

My Child is based on the most up-to-date information available within the health service, and on the experience and knowledge of child health and support services, voluntary organisations and parent groups. Each child is special and unique. Whether you are a new parent or you have done this before, we want to help you every step of the way.

As your baby grows and becomes a toddler, their personality will be starting to develop. You can support them to grow to be a healthy, strong, resilient and confident child. All of the information in these books, and more, is online at mychild.ie. We are so grateful to everyone who helped to create these books, especially the parents.

> This book is the second in a set of three books for parents:
>
> - My Pregnancy
> - My Child: 0 to 2 years
> - My Child: 2 to 5 years

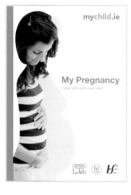 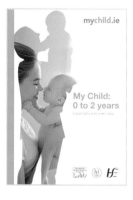 

Health checks for your child

From birth until the age of 2, you and your baby will usually have 11 planned appointments for healthcare checks and support.

Health checks are usually with your GP or your public health nurse. These visits are a great opportunity for you to talk about how you are getting on and ask any questions you have about yourself or your child.

Your child will also get vaccines to protect them from different infections. These vaccines and health checks are provided free of charge through the HSE.

Did you know?

Every child under the age of 6 can get a GP visit card. This means you can take your child to visit your GP for free. The GP visit card also covers them for free assessments at age 2 and 5. It also covers care for children with asthma.

You will get reminders about your child's next check. If you have changed your address, please tell your local health centre.

When	What happens at the health check
After birth, usually in hospital	**Newborn check and screening** A midwife will do an immediate check of your baby at birth. This will be done close to you. **Newborn clinical examination** Within the first 72 hours after birth, a doctor or midwife with specialist training will also examine your baby. **Hearing test (newborn hearing screening)** Your baby will also have their hearing checked.
During the first week	**Heel prick (newborn bloodspot screening)** In the first week after your baby is born, you will be offered newborn bloodspot screening. This is also called a heel prick. This may be done by the midwife in the hospital, or by your public health nurse at home. They will gently prick your baby's heel to collect some drops of blood onto a special card. Your baby will be screened to see if they are at risk of a number of rare conditions.
Within 72 hours of discharge from hospital or following a home birth	**Meet your public health nurse** Your public health nurse (PHN) will visit you at home to meet and support you and your family. They will usually weigh and examine your baby. The PHN will give advice on feeding, parenting and any questions you may have. They will talk to you about how to keep your baby safe when sleeping. They will also give you general tips about child safety. Check with your public health nurse about any baby clinics at the local HSE health centre. You may be able to call in and have your baby weighed at these clinics.
At 2 weeks	**2 week baby check** Make an appointment with your GP for a 2 week baby check. During this check your GP or the GP practice nurse will examine your baby. This is another opportunity to talk about your baby's wellbeing.

When	What happens at the health check
At 6 weeks – for you	**6 week check for you**
	Make an appointment with your GP for the 6 week check. This check is for both you and for your baby.
	Blood pressure
	Your GP may check your blood pressure, particularly if you had problems with this during your pregnancy.
	Stitches and wounds
	If you had stitches after the birth, your GP may check them. If you had a caesarean birth, they may check your wound.
	Cervical screening test
	Talk to your GP if:
	• you have never had a cervical screening test (smear test)
	• it is more than 3 years since you had one
	You may be eligible for a free cervical screening test. If you are eligible, this is normally done at least 3 months after the birth.
	Contraception
	Ask your GP about contraception if you are not planning to become pregnant at this time. See page 19.
	Your mood
	Your GP will ask you about your mood and how you are feeling. This is to see if you have any symptoms of postnatal depression, which is very common. See page 23. Your GP is there to support you. Do not be afraid to be open and honest with them about how you are feeling as they will be able to help.

When	What happens at the health check
At 6 weeks – for your baby	**6 week check for your baby** Your GP will ask how you and your baby are getting on and if you have any concerns. Parents know their baby best so feel free to discuss any aspect of your baby and their care. They will examine your baby from head to toe. They will also check on their hips, heart, eyes and, for boys, testicles. If you were told at birth that your baby needed a hip ultrasound, then you should have an appointment by now. If you haven't, tell your GP. If your GP can't feel one of your baby boy's testicles, then they will need to be checked again at 6 months of age. This is normally done by a paediatrician. If your GP cannot feel both testicles, they will arrange for an appointment with a paediatrician.
At 2 months	**Vaccines** Make an appointment with your GP or GP practice nurse for your baby's first vaccines. This is also called immunisation. See page 102 for more details.
At 3 months	**Developmental check** The public health nurse (PHN) will organise a developmental check for your baby. This will take place in the health centre or in your home. They will check your baby's growth and development. See page 125. They will talk to you about feeding your baby and give you advice about weaning (see page 59). Your PHN will also talk to you about child safety and give you a child safety wall chart and check-list.
At 4 months	**Vaccines** Make an appointment with your GP or GP practice nurse for your baby's second set of vaccines.
At 6 months	**Vaccines** Make an appointment with your GP or GP practice nurse for your baby's third set of vaccines.

When	What happens at the health check
At 9 to 11 months	**Developmental check** Your public health nurse or community medical doctor will talk to you about your child and any concerns that you have. They will also check your child's general health. This includes their teeth, development and growth. Your public health nurse or community medical doctor will talk to you about child safety as your baby may now be on the move. If you or your public health nurse or community medical doctor are concerned about any part of the check, then you and your child will be: • invited back for a re-check, or • referred to a specialist for further assessment
12 months	**Vaccines** Make an appointment with your GP or GP practice nurse for your baby's fourth set of vaccines.
13 months	**Vaccines** Make an appointment with your GP or GP practice nurse for the fifth set of vaccines. It takes five visits to fully vaccinate your child.
At 21 to 24 months	**Developmental check** Your public health nurse will talk to you about your child and any concerns that you have. They will also check your child's general health. This includes their teeth, development and growth. Your public health nurse will talk to you about child safety. If you or your public health nurse are concerned about any part of your child's check, then they may check them again or refer your child to a community medical doctor.

Taking care of yourself as a parent

Many people say that becoming a parent is one of the most challenging and rewarding experiences. It is important to take care of yourself during this time of change.

Your new life and your new role

You will need time to recover from the birth, to rest and to get to know your baby. You will also need time and support to adjust to your new role as a parent.

Developing your own parenting style

As your baby grows, you will be building patterns and routines that work well for their sleeping, eating and bedtime routines. You will be developing your own parenting style that supports your family.

During the first 2 years of your baby's life, you will get a lot of advice from family and friends. You will get to know your baby better than anyone else, so trust your instincts.

Love and attention

The most important thing you can give your growing baby is your love and attention. This includes:

- spending time getting to know them
- developing routines
- building positive relationships

Many parents work outside the home so the time you spend with your baby is important – every moment matters.

Dealing with tiredness

While caring for a small child is rewarding, it can be very tiring.

Try to get support from your partner or a family member to help with the housework so you have time to focus on your relationship with your baby.

Sleep deprivation

Sleep deprivation can be difficult. Your days and nights will become easier over time from about 6 weeks on. This is when your baby starts to settle into a routine for feeding and sleeping.

But when your baby begins teething at around 6 to 9 months old, sleepless nights may be back again.

Support

If you feel all of this is getting to be too much, then talk with your partner about ways you can both manage through this time.

You may not have a partner to turn to or you may need extra support. Talk to your GP, public health nurse or Tusla (the Child and Family Agency). They may suggest ways to get extra help. See page 28 for details of extra support.

Ready to bond

From the moment they are born, your baby is ready to form a relationship with you. They love looking at your face and getting to know you. This early relationship is very important for their development. Through you, they are learning about the world.

Give yourself time to build and nurture that positive relationship with your baby. Don't worry – a pattern will form in your daily routine that you are able to manage.

Rest and relaxation

Rest is important for parents, especially after your baby is born. In the first few days at home, try to:

- limit the number of visitors to your home
- have a rest or a sleep when your baby sleeps
- ask for and accept help with routine shopping or housework
- allow some of the housework to go undone for now and focus on your baby and yourself
- prepare and freeze meals ahead of time to cut down on daily housework

Your time

You may also feel that you have very little time for yourself since your baby was born. It is important to look after your own needs. This means you will be better able to look after the needs of your family. Take time out for yourself:

- Ask your partner or a family member to look after your child while you have a short rest.
- Go for a walk or a swim.
- Treat yourself to little things such as meeting friends for coffee, a new magazine, a bath.

You are learning on the job. Don't expect too much of yourself and those around you. Trust your instincts and know that you are doing your best.

Did you know?

Parent and toddler groups are when parents and carers come together with their children. This gives an opportunity for children to play and for adults to meet and talk.

Families come in all shapes and sizes

No matter what your family structure is, children do well when they are loved and cared for in a safe and supportive environment. What matters to children is how they are parented and supported as they grow and develop.

All parents face challenges. But some parents may face additional challenges due to their family structure.

Parenting as a couple

As you adjust to family life, your relationship can change. Your relationship may strengthen as you get to know your child together. Occasionally tension can arise, especially when one or both of you feel tired and stressed. You may find you have different opinions about certain aspects of parenting.

Work out how you will share things including:

- getting up at night to feed your child
- sharing the housework or shopping
- bathing and feeding your child
- taking time off work to care for your child when they are sick

It is common for new mothers not to feel like having sex for a while after the birth.

The important thing is that you and your partner talk to each other about your needs.

Same-sex couples

Parents in same-sex couples face the same challenges as all other parents. There may be some additional challenges such as discrimination or lack of understanding. Chat to your child and explain that families come in different shapes and sizes.

Taking care of your relationship

- Make time for each other – try and do things as a couple.
- Talk openly together and share your feelings in a calm and listening way.
- Share the household jobs.
- Allow your partner to develop their own style of parenting.
- Avoid arguing in front of your child.
- Have individual time with your child – this will strengthen your bond with your child while giving the other parent a break.

Shared parenting for parents who live apart

Parents have a very important role in their child's life, no matter what kind of relationship they are in. Shared parenting lets your child build a positive and loving relationship with both parents.

Tips include:

Keep in touch

Support your child to contact their other parent when at home. Encourage this contact when they are with their other parent. They can keep in contact through phone calls or online, for example Skype calls.

Make both homes feel special

Your child needs to feel at home in both parents' homes. They need both families to love and accept them.

Simple things can help. Let your child have a place for their own toothbrush, special blanket and toys. This is a sign that they belong and are not just passing through.

Parent together

Sometimes you may have a difficult relationship with the other parent. Try not to let this affect your child's relationship with the other parent.

As far as possible, both parents should try to stick to the same rules and approach to parenting.

Parenting alone

There are over 200,000 one parent families in Ireland today. Children thrive when they are loved and cared for.

- Take time to adjust and adapt to this role – remember that we all learn on the job when it comes to parenting.
- Focus on your strengths and skills.
- It is not easy to be a parent so have realistic expectations of yourself.
- Be kind to yourself – you have a lot to organise and a lot of responsibility.
- Make sure you make some time for yourself and the things you like to do.
- We all need help and support – don't be afraid to ask for help and support from family and friends.

Parenting after your partner dies

The death of a partner is a very difficult and emotional time for you and your family. If you are in this situation, you may feel unable to cope. You may feel uncertain about the future that you had planned together.

Help your child to understand what has happened by explaining it to them in a way that is appropriate for their age. Talk to your GP. They can provide you with information on local bereavement support services. They can also help you to work through some of the difficult emotions you may be experiencing at this time. See citizensinformation.ie for advice if you have been bereaved.

Older parents

Many parents are having children later in life for many reasons. There are both benefits and challenges to having children at any age. At an older age you may have more financial stability and support than you would have had in your 20s and 30s.

Despite this you face the same challenges as any parent. You may have extra challenges. Your own parents might be elderly or unwell or you may have teenage children.

All parents struggle with energy levels, especially when children are younger and sleep is an issue. All parents need help and support at different times. It is good to talk to parents with children of similar ages as your child. You will be able to share common experiences and challenges. You can get support, advice and friendship.

Younger parents

As a younger parent, you face similar challenges to any other parent. There may be additional challenges. You might worry about balancing family life with education and finding work. On the other hand, younger parents probably have more energy to deal with the demands of a young child.

- Consider staying with your parents if they are supporting you.
- If you are living on your own, find out what benefits or entitlements you can get. See citizensinformation.ie
- There may also be local community supports for parents. Your public health nurse will have information on these.
- Speak to other parents and parents the same age as you if possible.
- Like any parent, you will need to take a break - ask your family and friends for help.
- If you are in school or college, talk to a teacher you trust. This will help them to understand that you have other priorities as well as your education.
- Talking to your partner, family member or trusted friend can help you deal with the ups and downs of being a parent.

Becoming parents after fertility treatments

Many parents need fertility treatments to help them to become pregnant. Your journey towards becoming a parent may have been a difficult, expensive and stressful time. Looking after a baby or small child can be exciting and bring great joy. But there is no doubt that it can be challenging at times.

Sometimes if you have had IVF or other treatments you may feel guilty when you are stressed and tense. Sometimes you may feel that you should not complain. All new parents need support, no matter how they became parents.

For couples who are separating or divorcing

Separation or divorce can be stressful for a family. It is normal for you and your child to be upset. You will need to balance dealing with your own emotions and looking after the needs of your child.

Caring for yourself during a separation or divorce

- Get support and help from others, such as family and friends.
- Look after yourself. Eat, sleep, rest, take exercise and reduce the amount of alcohol you drink.
- Keep telling yourself that this upsetting time will pass.
- Be positive about your future. Make realistic plans for yourself and your children.
- Contact organisations like Tusla (the Child and Family Agency), which offer family mediation and counselling services. These services can help to ease your stress and fears and have a positive impact on your child.

Helping your child through a separation or divorce

- Love, support and reassure your child.
- Explain why you are separating or divorcing. Reassure your child that it is because of difficulties in your relationship as a couple and it is not their fault.
- Both parents need to give the same explanation in a way that is suitable for your child's age.
- Talk to other adults who are involved in caring for your child. It is important that they are made aware of any big changes in your child's home life.
- Listen to your child's feelings and the reasons they are angry or sad. Sit down with them so it is easy to make eye contact. Eye contact lets them know that you are listening to them.
- Try and spend individual time with each child. Simply spending time with your child can encourage them to talk.
- Encourage them to spend time with their friends doing normal things like playing.

What to say:

- Tell your child that they can still love both parents. They don't have to take sides.
- Tell your child that it's ok to talk about their feelings, worries or anger.
- Respect your child – tell them about the process and involve them in decisions as much as you can.
- Do not speak badly about your partner and why you are separating, despite how you may feel. Your child may feel guilty about loving their other parent while they try to be loyal to you.

You may need extra support

If you or your child are finding it hard to cope, there are professionals who can help.

There is a range of support services available:

- Citizens Information Centre: 0761 07 4000 and citizensinformation.ie
- COSC (The National Office for the Prevention of Domestic, Sexual and Gender-based Violence): whatwouldyoudo.ie
- Money Advice and Budgeting Service (MABS): 0761 07 2000 and mabs.ie
- Barnardos: 01 453 0355 and barnardos.ie
- Your GP
- Your public health nurse
- Social work services from tusla.ie.

See page 28.

Especially for mothers after the birth

Eating well

It can take time for your body to recover from pregnancy and birth. To help you recover, eat healthily and exercise regularly. Going on a weight loss diet is not recommended just after you have given birth, especially if you are breastfeeding.

Healthy eating is always important, especially after giving birth.

- Use the food pyramid to help you choose a daily balanced diet – choose 3 servings of dairy products like milk, cheese and yoghurt every day.
- Eat foods high in fibre to avoid constipation, especially if you had stitches or bruising. Examples include vegetables, fruit and wholemeal or wholegrain varieties of bread, cereals, pasta or rice.
- Aim to drink at least 8 to 10 glasses of water a day. If you are breastfeeding you will need 11 to 14 glasses of water a day.

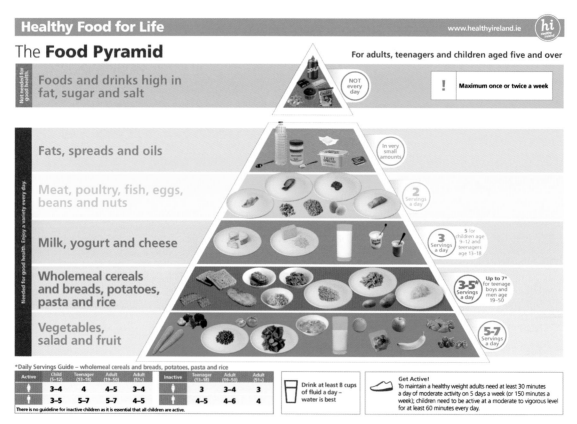

Source: Department of Health, December 2016.

Smoking and drinking alcohol

If you gave up smoking during your pregnancy, you gave your baby a great start. Try to stay off cigarettes as smoking around your baby increases their risk of cot death.

Quitting smoking is one of the best ways to protect your own health and wellbeing. Free help and support that can double your chances of quitting is available from the HSE on quit.ie.

See askaboutalcohol.ie for information on alcohol and your health. For advice about drinking alcohol while breastfeeding, see page 36.

Physical activity

Just as it took time to grow your pregnancy, it will take time for your body to recover. Try and be patient and be kind to yourself. Taking regular physical exercise is good for your general health and will improve your sense of wellbeing.

Some gentle exercises can help increase your energy levels and help you manage the added work in your life following the birth of your baby.

Build physical activity into your daily routine by going for a walk with your baby. Inviting someone along gives you a chance to spend time together. Go swimming once you feel ready. You may need to wait for any stitches to heal and bleeding to stop.

Pelvic floor exercises

Pelvic floor exercises are when you squeeze the muscles around your vagina and anus to strengthen them. It is important to begin pelvic floor muscle exercises as soon as possible after the birth of your baby.

These are important to prevent future health problems such as leakage of urine (incontinence). Your midwife or physiotherapist will give you information about how to do pelvic floor muscle exercises.

Do these exercises regularly. If you had a caesarean birth, a physiotherapist will give you information on suitable exercises.

Contraception

It is possible to become pregnant again soon after the birth of your baby, even if your periods have not returned. If you do not want to get pregnant now, you and your partner can decide on a method of family planning that suits you both.

You can get information on family planning and contraception from your midwife, GP, public health nurse or GP practice nurse. See sexualwellbeing.ie

The baby blues

Soon after the birth of your baby it is normal to feel very tearful and emotional. You may find it is hard to explain why you are crying, or why you feel upset. This is called the baby blues. See page 22.

A new brother or sister in the family

This is a time of change for older children in your family. While they may be excited by a new brother or sister, they may feel jealous at times.

An older child may go back to baby behaviour for a time, such as wanting a bottle or breastfeed, or asking to be lifted up. It will take time and patience to cope with the extra demands.

There are ways to help them to adjust to their new brother or sister:

- If possible, spend some individual time with your older child. This may help to make them feel secure and adjust to their new position in their family.

- Encourage your older child or children to become involved in caring for your baby. If this does not happen, don't try to force it. This will happen in time.

- Talk to your older child about how great it is becoming a big brother or sister.

- Don't make any major changes to your older child's life. For example, do not start potty training or stop the use of soothers shortly after your new baby's arrival.

- Breastfeeding may be a time when your older child may feel excluded. It's a good idea to have a special box of toys or books that you bring out during breastfeeding for them to play with.

- It may be possible to tandem feed (breastfeeding your baby and an older child) for a while. You can get more information about this from your local breastfeeding group. See page 42.

Caring for twins or more

Bringing your babies home from hospital is both an exciting and daunting experience.

In the early days you may miss the support of the hospital. Your GP and public health nurse are there to support you. You can also phone the hospital where you gave birth for more help.

Feeding

You will get support in the hospital on how to breastfeed twins. It is possible to breastfeed when you have more than one baby. It has lots of health benefits for you and your babies. Breastfeeding can also be a great help in soothing your babies. It also helps you to build a strong bond with them.

Dividing your attention between 2 or more babies can feel overwhelming at times. You may want to express and store your milk so your partner can help you with the feeds.

If you have decided to formula feed, you will be given information on making feeds.

Some mothers find feeding both babies at the same time easier. This is called tandem feeding.

Tips for twins and multiple babies

- Develop a routine that suits you around the basic needs of your babies – feeding, sleeping and playing.
- Make feeding a special time where you start to build a relationship with your babies.
- Take time to talk to your babies and learn from their signals when they want to be fed and when they have had enough.
- Include your other children – for example, making time for storytelling.
- There is no need to bathe your babies every day – 2 or 3 times a week is fine.
- Bathe your babies on alternative nights to make it a special time. This helps you to spend good quality time with each baby and get to know their personalities.
- Accept offers of help from family and friends so you can rest and have some time for yourself.
- Make your home a no smoking zone – do not let anyone smoke around your babies, no matter where they are.

Support

Your midwives, public health nurse, GP or maternity hospital are there to help.

The Irish Multiple Births Association has information and support on a range of topics for parents of twins, triplets or more. See imba.ie or phone 01 874 9056.

Baby blues and postnatal depression

Pregnancy and giving birth are deeply emotional experiences. Having a newborn baby is exhilarating, exhausting and physically challenging.

The sense of responsibility can be daunting. You may have feelings of inadequacy and guilt. This can feel overwhelming.

Many mothers feel changes in their emotions and mood at some point in their pregnancy and in the first few weeks after birth. This is a normal part of adjusting to the changes of becoming a mother.

Baby blues

The baby blues are very common and considered normal. It happens to about 80% of women. Most new mothers feel baby blues a few days after the birth. They usually begin 2 to 3 days after the birth. They are sometimes called the '2 day tears' or the 'day 3 blues'.

The baby blues are linked to the sudden drop of hormones that you experience after giving birth. On top of all these hormonal changes, you are trying to get used to a new baby. It can take a few days for your hormones to realign after giving birth.

Signs of baby blues

You might be more tearful and emotional than normal. You may be irritable. You might feel isolated, vulnerable and lonely. You can also feel "high" and elated or very happy during this time.

How long the baby blues last

Although you may find them distressing while you have them, the baby blues will pass quickly. They usually pass after a few days or after 1 week.

Finding support

Allow yourself to cry. Most new mothers experience the baby blues. Your body needs rest. Try to have at least one proper rest in bed each day.

Talk to a person close to you, like a partner, family member or close friend. You will need support to help you get as much rest as you can.

When to get help

If your baby blues last for more than 1 week, it may be a sign that you are at risk of postnatal depression. Talk to your midwife, public health nurse or GP. They can help you.

Postnatal depression

Postnatal depression is depression that some women have in the first year after having a baby. It is common.

> ## Did you know?
>
> Up to 1 in 5 women in Ireland have postnatal depression in the months after giving birth.
>
> Your family and friends may notice that you have postnatal depression before you do. The most important thing is to get help.

Signs and symptoms of postnatal depression

Symptoms of postnatal depression may start as baby blues and then get worse. The symptoms may take some time to develop. Postnatal depression may be most obvious when your baby is 4 to 6 months old.

You may be feeling sad, angry and alone. You may feel like you have no interest in yourself or in the baby. You may have anxiety. You may even have panic attacks where you have a fast heartbeat, feel dizzy or sick and are sweating. You may not want to spend time with people, even your baby.

Other symptoms of postnatal depression include:

- crying easily
- feeling rejected by your baby
- worrying a lot about your baby
- feeling afraid to be alone with your baby
- loss of appetite
- feeling inadequate
- feeling tired all the time
- problems sleeping (insomnia)
- loss of interest in sex
- difficulty concentrating
- negative thoughts like "I am a bad mother"

Get help from your GP or public health nurse if:

- these feelings or symptoms last for more than 2 weeks, or
- you have any thoughts of harming yourself or your baby

You will feel like yourself again

The most important thing you can do is ask for help. Talk to your partner, family and friends. Talk to your GP or public health nurse. Try to explain to them exactly how you feel. Trust that you will feel like yourself again.

Eat well and try and get some exercise. Ask family and friends for help. Don't put too much pressure on yourself with housework and other chores. Focus on yourself and your baby.

Your GP may refer you for counselling or may prescribe medication. Remind your GP if you are breastfeeding. Some medication is not suitable for women who are breastfeeding.

If you show symptoms of postnatal depression, your public health nurse will tell you what support is available in your area.

It is not your fault

There is often no obvious reason for postnatal depression. You may feel guilty about this. You may find yourself thinking that you should be happy about having a baby. Postnatal depression can happen to anyone. This is not your fault.

Getting help

If it is not treated, postnatal depression can last for months or even years. The earlier it is recognised, diagnosed and treated, the faster you will recover.

Some women may feel too scared, guilty or embarrassed to look for help. You may not want to talk about struggling with your feelings when a new baby has arrived. By getting help, you are doing what is best for you and for your baby.

Your GP and public health nurse will want to give you the care you need to recover and be able to look after your baby.

It is routine for your GP and public health nurse to ask you questions about your mood. It's good to answer these questions honestly so that they can give you the support you need. With these types of supports you will start to feel better.

There are very effective treatments for postnatal depression. These include:

- listening and support
- recommending local community supports, like mother and baby groups
- referring you to a counsellor
- medication
- referring you to a specialist if needed

Self help

Along with getting help from your GP or public health nurse, there are also some things you can do to help you feel better.

Do:

✔ Eat well – try not to skip meals.

✔ Get rest whenever possible.

✔ Talk to someone you trust about how you are feeling.

✔ Let others help you with housework or looking after older children.

✔ Try to spend time doing things that help you to relax, like listening to music or going for a walk.

✔ Try to spend time with your partner and loved ones.

✔ Ask your public health nurse if there are any mother and baby groups in your area. Although you may not feel like going, the support of other new mothers can really help.

✔ Be as active as you can.

Don't:

✗ Be afraid – postnatal depression is common and very treatable. You will feel like you again.

✗ Blame yourself or your partner – this is no-one's fault and can happen to anyone after birth.

✗ Try to do everything yourself – you may have to lower your standards on housework and other chores when you have a new baby.

✗ Use alcohol or drugs to help you feel better. They can make depression worse.

When to get help urgently

Talk to your GP, local out of hours GP service or hospital emergency department (A&E) immediately if:

• you have thoughts about harming yourself or your baby, or

• you have unusual symptoms like hearing voices or unusual beliefs – for example, that people are out to get you or that you have committed a crime

1 in 5 women will have a mental health problem during pregnancy or in the first year after giving birth. This could be a previous problem that has resurfaced or the first time you have experienced a mental health problem.

How partners, friends and families can help

When someone you love has postnatal depression, it can be an extremely worrying time. This is an illness, like any physical illness. It happens to up to 1 in every 5 mothers.

Like most illnesses, it can take time to recover from postnatal depression. If you feel you do not understand what postnatal depression is, talk to your public health nurse or GP.

Know the signs

Postnatal depression responds well to treatment. It is important that your loved one with postnatal depression gets treatment as soon as possible. Know the signs and symptoms (see page 23) of postnatal depression so you know when to encourage her to get help.

Be there

Simply being there, offering your time, support and encouragement can really help a person who is depressed. Listen to her. Reassure her that she will get better.

Help her to get help

Many mothers with postnatal depression are reluctant to get help. This is for lots of reasons.

Reassure her

Tell her how common postnatal depression is. Tell her that she needs help, and that she will feel better soon. Listen to her. What are her concerns? Offer to go with her to the GP if she would like.

Know when to get help urgently

Always make sure that anyone with postnatal depression gets help quickly if they talk about harming themselves or the baby. She will need to be seen urgently by her GP. Do not delay.

Encourage her to see the GP and go with her. If she does not agree to go, contact your GP for advice on what to do.

Help her to look after herself

Make sure she gets enough rest. Prepare food and snacks to encourage her to eat. Encourage her to go for a walk or take some form of exercise, as this is proven to help with depression.

Practical help

Help with housework, shopping, cooking and caring for the baby. Postnatal depression can mean that even simple tasks can feel overwhelming at times. If she has older children, take them out for a while.

Give her a break

Take the baby out for a walk to give her some time to herself. Encourage her to see her friends and family.

Try not to be angry with her or with the baby

It's hard not to blame the baby sometimes when the person you love becomes depressed after the birth. It is normal for partners to feel resentful towards the baby and towards the woman with postnatal depression.

You may feel like your needs have been pushed to one side. It is understandable to feel this way. The most important thing is for the mother to get well again. If she gets the help and support she needs, she will recover more quickly.

Look after yourself

Take care of yourself too – life with a new baby is stressful, especially if the baby's mother is unwell with postnatal depression.

- Find someone to talk to.
- Take some time for yourself – you need a break too.

Did you know?

Research has shown that up to 10% of partners experience depression after a baby is born. Speak to your GP if you are feeling down, depressed or anxious for more than 2 weeks.

Getting extra support

There may be times when you need extra support from professionals to help your child and your family. You are not alone in looking for help. Other parents need extra support at times too.

Getting extra support is a smart thing to do. It shows that you value your family.

You may need extra support if you:

- are unsure what to expect because this is your first baby
- do not have a partner or a support person to share the joy and the work of being a parent
- find that your relationship with your partner is in difficulty
- feel there is support for your baby and your partner but little support for you
- now live away from home and family

There is a wide range of services available to help you and your family when you need it. Some of these services are outlined below.

Public health nurses

Public health nurses (PHNs) are there to help you and your family. They have experience in child and family health. They give information, advice and support to parents.

For example, your PHN can give advice about your child's:

- feeding
- development
- wellbeing
- special needs or long-term illness

Your PHN can also refer you to other local sources of support. These include:

- a parent and baby group or parent and toddler group
- the community mothers' programme
- breastfeeding support groups
- parenting classes
- support services offered by the HSE and other organisations

GPs and GP practice nurses

Your GP (general practitioner) is a family doctor. They probably cared for you during your pregnancy. GPs deal with a large range of health needs.

They also provide health education. They can give you advice on smoking and lifestyle. Many GPs also offer family planning services. Some perform minor procedures.

Your GP practice nurse works with your GP to give care to you and your family.

In many GP practices, the practice nurse gives children their vaccines.

GPs usually offer a private service (where you pay a fee). Most also provide services for the HSE where patients with a medical card or GP visit card get GP visits free of charge.

> All children under the age of 6 are entitled to a GP visit card (see page 216). This means you don't have to pay when you bring your child to the GP.
>
> Your child's vaccines are also provided free of charge by GPs for the HSE.

Tusla – the Child and Family Agency

Tusla provides support to families through their:

- family resource centres
- child and family support networks

See tusla.ie or phone 01 771 8500. Tusla's parenting24seven.ie has tips on parenting.

Ask for professional help if:

- you or your partner feel unhappy in your relationship, or
- there is conflict between you and you argue in front of your children

Tusla has links with voluntary organisations around the country that offer:

- parenting programmes
- Meitheal – a community-based support service for families
- child and family support networks
- marriage counselling
- child counselling
- child bereavement counselling and support
- family mediation – a free and confidential service that helps parents who have decided to separate or divorce

Social work services

Social work services are for children and families who sometimes need extra support to do their best for their family. Tusla's social work teams are in place in every community. They provide a wide range of preventative and child protection services.

Social workers work closely with parents and children to find out what their needs are and to develop a plan to meet those needs. Contact details for social workers are available on tusla.ie or by phoning 01 771 8500.

Barnardos

Barnardos helps children and families who need extra support at times. Their services include:

- family support in partnership with the HSE
- bereavement counselling for children
- information, training and a range of leaflets and books for parents and people who work with children

For more information call 01 435 0355 or see barnardos.ie

HSE Community Psychology Services

Your GP and other professionals can give you information on your local child, adolescent and family psychology service. They can make a referral for you if necessary.

Feeding your baby

Feeding helps your child to be nourished and to grow strong and healthy. There may be challenges but there is support and help available.

Talk to your public health nurse if you have any concerns about feeding. See page 42 for information on breastfeeding support.

Responsive feeding

Responsive parenting is an important part of forming a healthy relationship with your baby. It means that you are responding sensitively to your baby while accepting their needs and signals.

This type of parenting helps your baby to form healthy brain connections and encourages feelings of safety and comfort. Your baby loves when you hold them close. It comforts your baby and helps them feel secure.

You can do responsive feeding by responding to your baby when they are showing signs of:

- hunger (early feeding cues) – see page 32
- distress

Tips for responsive breastfeeding

- Feed your baby whenever they show signs of wanting to breastfeed. Respond to your baby's early feeding cues. Do not try to time the feeds or feed to a schedule.

- Remember that you are not 'spoiling' your baby by responding to their needs in this way.

Tips for responsive bottle-feeding

- Your baby will love it if you or your partner do most of the feeds – they know you best.
- Gently encourage the baby to root and invite them to take the teat.
- Pace the feed or go at your baby's pace – try not to rush. Never force your baby to take a full feed.

Did you know?

It's normal for babies to lose weight in the first few days after birth. After this they begin gaining weight and by 2 weeks of age they are usually back at their birth weight.

Breastfeeding

Your breast milk is all your baby needs for the first 6 months and it is then part of their wider diet as they grow.

Breastfeeding is soothing and comforting for your baby and creates a special closeness. It gives you a chance to rest with your baby and to get to know them.

Breastfeeding:

- protects your health and your baby's health
- is important for your baby's healthy growth and development
- provides antibodies to protect your baby from illness and build their immune system
- helps you to be a healthy weight
- reduces your risk of breast cancer, ovarian cancer and diabetes

Breastfeeding helps protect your baby from:

- ear, chest, nose and tummy infections
- obesity (being very overweight)
- diabetes
- cot death

Early feeding cues

It is best to feed your baby when they show signs of being hungry. These are called early feeding cues. Cues include:

- eyes fluttering or moving over and back, even if their eyelids are closed
- moving their hands to their mouth or towards their face
- opening and closing their mouth
- 'rooting' — turning their head when you touch their cheek, or trying to move towards your breast
- making cooing noises

Crying is a late sign of hunger or late feeding cue. Try feeding when you notice the earlier signs. It will be easier as you will both be calmer and more relaxed.

Breastfeeding positions

Before you start breastfeeding, find a comfortable position. There are very few rules but it is important that you and your baby are positioned comfortably.

Have a glass of water close to hand, and perhaps a snack. Like any new skill, breastfeeding takes practice. See mychild.ie for step-by-step guides on different breastfeeding positions.

Attaching your baby to your breast

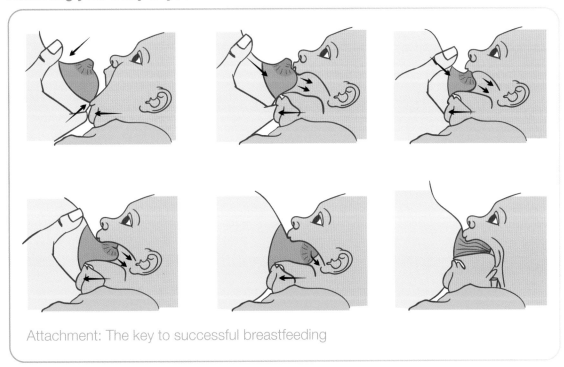

Attachment: The key to successful breastfeeding

Positioning and attachment is about how you hold your baby at your breast so they can feed. This is also called latching on. Proper positioning and attachment is the most important thing for successful breastfeeding.

When your baby is well positioned and attached, they will find it easier to feed well and you will find it more comfortable.

In the early days, you may feel sensitive at the beginning of a feed as you get used to the new feeling. Feeding should not be painful.

Get help with positioning and attaching from your public health nurse, midwife, lactation consultant or voluntary breastfeeding organisation if you continue to feel discomfort.

Follow these steps to position and attach your baby well.

1. Hold your baby close with their nose level with your nipple.
2. Let your baby's head tip back so their top lip brushes against your nipple — this should help them open their mouth wide.

3. When your baby's mouth is wide open, bring them to your breast.

4. Aim your nipple to the roof of their mouth.

5. When they attach, your nipple and most of the areola (the area around your nipple) should be deep in your baby's mouth.

6. When your baby is attached properly, their chin will be pressed into your breast.

7. Your baby's nose should be clear for easy breathing. Ideally, the nose should be at a tilt when attached correctly.

8. If your baby's nose appears to be blocked, move their bottom closer to you. This will create a head tilt and free up their nose.

9. The deeper the attachment, the more comfortable you will feel and the better your baby will feed.

How to know your baby is attached correctly

Signs that your baby is attached correctly:

Head position

- Your baby should have a wide mouthful of breast in their mouth.
- More of your areola will be visible above their top lip than below their bottom lip.
- Their chin should be touching your breast.
- You may notice their top and bottom lips curled out.
- Their cheeks should be full and rounded, you should not see the cheeks dimpling when baby sucks.
- Their jaw should be moving, you may also see their ears twitch as they feed.

Sucks and sounds

- They will start with short quick sucks, then change to long deep sucks with pauses to breathe.
- You should hear them swallowing as your breast milk volume increases.
- You should not hear smacking or clicking sounds.

Calm and comfortable

- They should feed calmly and not move on and off the breast.
- You will feel comfortable during a feed and your nipples should not be sore.
- When they finish feeding, they should seem satisfied.

Breastfeeding during the first 4 weeks

Newborn babies have tiny tummies. They can feed 10 to 12 times in 24 hours. Your milk is very easy for your baby to digest.

In the first few weeks, you and your baby are getting used to breastfeeding. This is called establishing breastfeeding.

Your supply of breast milk is established in the early weeks. This works by supply and demand. The more you breastfeed, the more milk your body produces.

To make sure you have a good supply of milk:

- Feed your baby often when they show early feeding cues.
- Let your baby feed as long as they wish.

When your baby is finished feeding, they will come off your breast. You can then offer your second breast. If your baby does not take this breast, offer it first at the next feed.

Feeding patterns

Some babies feed more at certain times of the day, often in the evening. This is normal.

> Breastfeeding is a skill that you and your baby will develop over the first few weeks. As the weeks pass, your baby may develop a more regular pattern of feeding. From around 4 weeks of age you and your baby will have breastfeeding well established.

Getting into a routine

You may start to notice that your day is falling into a fairly predictable routine. Every baby's pattern will differ, and it may change from time to time with occasional growth spurts. The longer they breastfeed, the easier it becomes.

It is normal for babies to wake at night for feeds. As your baby grows, they may settle and sleep for longer periods at night.

Breastfeeding at night gives your baby a large part of their calorie intake before they begin eating solid foods. It helps maintain your milk supply. Babies and toddlers also breastfeed for:

- comfort
- security
- warmth
- closeness
- familiarity

It is common for babies and toddlers to wake at night (see pages 79 to 81).

Soothers

Try not to give your baby a soother, dummy or dodie until breastfeeding is established, usually when your baby is 1 month old.

Using soothers has been shown to reduce the amount of breast milk your body makes. It may interfere with your baby attaching correctly onto your breast.

What to eat and drink

There's no need to follow a special diet when you are breastfeeding. Breastfeeding is thirsty work so make sure you are drinking plenty of water.

Being a new mother is busy and can be hard work. Try to have a healthy and balanced diet to make sure you are getting all of the nutrients you need.

A healthy and balanced diet means:

- at least 5 to 7 servings of vegetables, salad and fruit each day
- wholegrain bread, pasta, rice or potatoes
- plenty of fibre to prevent constipation — wholegrains, beans, lentils, fruit and vegetables
- protein such as lean meat, poultry, fish and eggs
- dairy foods such as milk, cheese and yoghurts

Try to have healthy snacks ready to grab for when you get hungry.

Examples include:

- fresh fruit
- yoghurts
- hummus and vegetables to dip like carrots and celery
- sandwiches
- dried fruit like raisins, apricots and prunes
- breakfast cereals or muesli that are fortified with vitamins
- baked beans on toast
- baked potato with cheese
- boiled eggs

What to avoid

Alcohol

It's best to avoid drinking alcohol until your baby is more than 1 month old. In the first few weeks, you and your baby are getting used to breastfeeding. This is called establishing breastfeeding.

If you choose to drink alcohol once breastfeeding is established, there are steps you can take to avoid passing alcohol to your baby through your milk:

- feed your baby before drinking alcohol
- express your breast milk if you plan to drink more than 2 standard drinks – 1 standard drink is a half a pint of beer, a single measure of spirits or a small glass of wine
- wait 2 hours after each standard drink before breastfeeding your baby

- do not drink more than 11 standard drinks a week
- spread your drinks over the week
- have at least 2 alcohol-free days per week

You may not be able to take care of your baby properly if you are affected by alcohol. Only time makes alcohol leave your body and your milk. Drinking water or expressing your breast milk will not clear the alcohol from your body any faster. Breastfeeding while there is alcohol in your breast milk can affect your baby's sleep.

Caffeine

Drinks containing caffeine like tea, coffee and energy drinks may keep your baby awake.

Keep your caffeine intake to less than 200 mg per day, the same as when you were pregnant.

Examples of foods and drinks containing caffeine include:

- 1 mug of filter coffee – 140 mg caffeine
- 1 mug of instant coffee – 100 mg caffeine
- 1 mug of tea – 75 mg caffeine
- 1 can of energy drink can have up to 160 mg caffeine, depending on the size
- 1 cola drink tends to have 40 mg caffeine

Fish

Oily fish contains special types of fat. These are called long chain omega fatty acids. These fats are really good for your baby's developing nervous system.

But some oily fish can contain low levels of pollutants. These can build up in your body. If you are breastfeeding, don't have more than two portions of oily fish each week.

You should not eat more than one portion of marlin, swordfish or shark per week. This is because these fish can contain high levels of mercury. There is no limit to how much tuna you can eat when breastfeeding.

Medication

Make sure any medicine, tablets or pills you take are safe for breastfeeding. Check with your GP, any doctor who is treating you or pharmacist.

Keep all medication out of your child's sight and reach.

Breastfeeding challenges

Breastfeeding is a skill that mothers and babies learn together. Like any skill, it takes practice and patience.

Things that help to prevent breastfeeding challenges:

- Feed your baby frequently when they show early feeding cues (see page 32).
- Make sure your baby is positioned and attached deeply onto your breast for comfort.

If you do have any breastfeeding challenges, you are not alone. Ask for help (see page 42). There is almost always a solution.

Sore or bleeding nipples

If your nipples are sore or bleeding, get help.

Ask your lactation consultant, public health nurse or GP practice nurse to check that your baby is correctly positioned and attached to the breast.

They will help you to:

- become more comfortable feeding
- treat sore nipples

If the position you use when feeding your baby or the way your baby is attached to your breast isn't the cause of the problem, they will advise you about treatment. Other causes may include tongue-tie (see page 41) or thrush (see page 40).

Tips

If the position you use when feeding your baby or the way your baby is attached to your breast is causing your problems, some of the following tips may help:

- After each feed, hand express (see page 44) some milk. Gently rub the milk into the nipple area. Let this dry before covering again.
- Gently massage your nipples with warm fingers and 100% lanolin nipple ointment – follow the instructions and make sure you are in a warm room.
- Spread a small amount of 100% lanolin nipple cream on a clean dry breastpad and place over the nipple. Change the breastpad frequently (read the instructions) to prevent moisture staying on your skin.
- Use a hydrogel compress – ask your pharmacist for advice on which types are suitable for breastfeeding women and follow the instructions.

If it feels too painful to feed, you could pump milk (see page 45) for a day or two. This gives your nipples time to heal. Hand expressing (page 44) may be more comfortable than using a pump.

Unsettled feeding

Unsettled feeding means your baby is fussing or crying at the breast.

Ask for help from your lactation consultant, public health nurse, midwife or neonatal nurse about the best ways to correctly position and attach your baby to your breast. When your baby has finished the first breast, try offering your second breast at each feed.

Engorgement

Breast engorgement is when your breasts get too full of milk. This can leave them feeling hard and painful.

Engorgement can happen in the early days of feeding. It can take a few days for your supply of breast milk to match what your baby needs. It can also happen later on, for example when you introduce solid foods to your baby and your baby starts to drink less breast milk.

Ask your public health nurse, GP practice nurse or lactation consultant for help if you think your breasts are engorged. They can show you how to express a little milk by hand before a feed to soften your breast and help your baby to attach (see page 33).

Other tips include:

- Wear a well-fitting bra designed for breastfeeding mothers (nursing bra).
- Apply warm flannels to your breasts before a feed or before you hand express.
- Keep cabbage leaves in the fridge and put them on your breasts after a feed.
- Take paracetamol or ibuprofen to help with the pain - ask your pharmacist for advice.

Blocked ducts

If you have a blocked duct, you will usually notice an area of your breast that is sore. You might feel a hard and tender lump when you press your breast. You will generally feel well.

A blocked duct can happen when the milk is not flowing freely from that milk duct in your breast. Causes can include wearing a bra that is too tight, incorrect positioning and attachment or missing a feed.

Mastitis

Mastitis means you have an inflammation in one of your breasts. This can happen when a blocked duct is not relieved. If you have mastitis, your breast can feel painful and inflamed. If mastitis is not treated, it can become infected and you will need to take antibiotics.

If you have mastitis, you may have:

- a red patch of skin on your breast that is painful to touch
- a high fever
- flu-like symptoms – feeling generally unwell, achy and tired

You may also feel tearful.

Ask your public health nurse, GP practice nurse, midwife, neonatal nurse, or lactation consultant to check that your baby is correctly positioned and attached to your breast.

Tips for blocked ducts and mastitis

Some tips to help a blocked duct or mastitis include:

- Feed more often and feed from the affected breast first.
- If your baby cannot feed, express from that side.
- Warm up your breast with a hot wet flannel before feeding.
- If you have mastitis only, cool your breast with a cold flannel after the feed.
- Massage your breast while your baby is feeding.
- Rest and take a painkiller like paracetamol or ibuprofen - ask your pharmacist for advice.

See your GP if there is no improvement after 12 to 24 hours or if things are getting worse.

Thrush

Usually the baby will get thrush first and pass it to their mother. Thrush is caused by candida, which is a type of yeast.

Symptoms

Symptoms include your nipples suddenly becoming sore and bright pink. Your nipple may be:

- shiny or flaky
- sore after a breastfeed or at night

Symptoms of thrush in your baby include:

- creamy white patches or white spots which cannot be removed in the mouth, on the tongue or in the cheeks
- their tongue or lips may have a white or pearly gloss
- a nappy rash – this happens to some babies

What to do

See your GP if you think you or your baby has thrush. Bring your baby with you. You will both need to be treated at the same time. Your GP may prescribe an ointment, cream or gel.

Other tips:

- You may take a probiotic to help the treatment – ask your pharmacist for advice.
- If using breast pads, make sure you change them after every feed.
- Make sure you and your family wash your hands properly — thrush can be passed on to the baby and other family members. Use separate towels.
- Wash clothes in a 60 degree wash.

- If you are expressing breast milk, do not freeze it. Wait until you have finished treatment and are symptom-free before you express milk for freezing.
- Go to your public health nurse, lactation consultant or local breastfeeding support group for help with positioning and attachment.

Tongue-tie

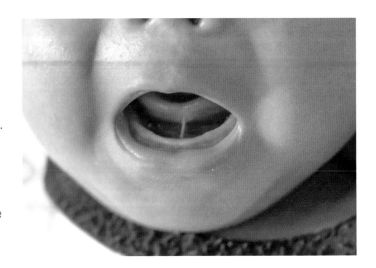

Some babies with tongue-tie are not able to move and stretch their tongues freely. This may interfere with positioning and attachment onto the breast.

What it is

Tongue-tie happens when the frenulum (the strip of skin that attaches the tongue to the base of the mouth) is too short, tight or thick.

Signs and difficulties

Tongue-tie can reduce the amount of breast milk your baby gets. It can also reduce your supply of breast milk.

Signs of tongue-tie include:

- difficulties in getting your baby properly attached to the breast and keeping them there
- your baby losing weight or having difficulty gaining weight
- restless, tiring and unsettled feeds
- noisy or clicking sounds during the feed
- dribbling of milk during feeds

Difficulties for mothers include:

- distorted nipple shape after a breastfeed
- nipple pain and bleeding, damaged or ulcerated nipples
- engorgement (where your breasts feel very full, and sometimes quite hard)
- mastitis

What to do

See your lactation consultant, public health nurse, midwife or GP if you think your baby has tongue-tie.

Better positioning and attachment can help with feeding challenges. Some babies may need a frenotomy. This is where the frenulum causing the tongue-tie is released in a minor operation.

Leaks

Sometimes breast milk may leak from your nipples. If you use breast pads, change them at every feed.

Support from others

Breastfeeding groups are a helpful way to meet other mothers and get information and support. Your public health nurse can give you the details of your nearest group or you can find them on mychild.ie

These groups are run by public health nurses or mothers who are trained to support breastfeeding.

Did you know?

The HSE provides an online service called Ask our Breastfeeding Expert - see mychild.ie. Lactation consultants are available to answer your questions. You can send a question by email, on Facebook, or you can live chat on our website.

Support is available from your midwife, neonatal nurse, public health nurse, GP, GP practice nurse and groups including:

- Cuidiú – cuidiu.ie
- La Leche League – lalecheleagueireland.com
- Friends of Breastfeeding – friendsofbreastfeeding.ie

How partners can help

All newborn babies need to feed frequently during the day and during the night. Your support can help your partner, especially when she is tired or experiencing challenges. Tips include:

- Ask her what she needs.
- Help her to position the baby near the breast to get ready for feeding — your midwife will support and guide you both.
- Ask family and friends to keep their visits short in the early days when you are both tired.
- Make healthy meals for your partner — feeding the mother is feeding the baby!
- Help out with housework.
- Plan something fun to do with any older children.

Breastfeeding when out and about

Breastfeeding is convenient when you are out and about with your baby. Your breast milk is always available and always at the right temperature. There is very little to organise for trips as you don't need bottles or feeding equipment.

Where you can breastfeed

You can breastfeed anywhere you and your baby wants and needs to. This is your right. You don't have to ask permission to breastfeed in any premises. Some places may offer a private area if you would like this, but you don't have to use it.

The Equal Status Act (2000) protects mothers from being discriminated against or harassed because they are breastfeeding in a public area.

What to wear

Wear trousers or a skirt with a jumper, sweatshirt or t-shirt that you can pull up from the waist. If possible wear a nursing bra that you can open from the front with one hand.

Look for cues

Don't wait until your baby gets too hungry or distressed. Feed your baby early and you will both be more relaxed and feeding will go smoothly.

Breastfeeding offers comfort as well as food. That's why breastfed babies are often more easily settled.

Expressing breast milk

Expressing means removing milk from your breast so you can store it and feed it to your baby later.

You remove the milk by hand or with a breast pump. In the first few days after the birth it is best to hand express. Expressing your breast milk is a very useful skill to learn.

In the early days, you may want to express milk if:

- Your baby needs to be cared for in a special care baby unit or paediatric hospital.
- You or your baby are too ill to breastfeed after birth.
- Your breasts feel very full or uncomfortable.
- Your baby is having difficulty attaching onto your breast.

As your baby grows, you may want to express milk when you are going to be away from your baby.

Expressing means that during the time you're away from your baby you will:

- be able to relieve the fullness in your breasts.
- have milk for your baby's carer.

Did you know?

When you express, it can be helpful to close your eyes and imagine your baby is feeding at your breast. Thinking of your baby or looking at a photo or video of them can help you relax and connect with your baby before you begin expressing. Having their clothing or blanket with you can also help.

If possible, spend some time together in skin-to-skin contact before you begin to express.

Hand-expressing breast milk

Getting ready

- Find a comfortable place to express.
- Minimise distractions.
- Wash your hands.
- Have everything you need to hand – for example, a drink of water, snack and a small towel.
- Think about your baby.
- Warm your breasts – take a warm shower or put a warm facecloth (warm compress or flannel) on your breasts.
- Massage your breasts before expressing – you can do this while in the shower.

Massage

Massage your breasts. This encourages the release of hormones and helps get your milk flowing.

1. Start by washing your hands in warm water.
2. Gently massage your breast.
3. This can be done with your fingertips (as shown in image A) or by rolling your closed fist over your breast towards the nipple (as shown in image B).
4. Work around the whole breast, including underneath. Don't slide your fingers along your breast as it can damage the skin.

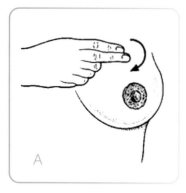
A

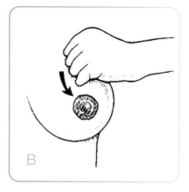
B

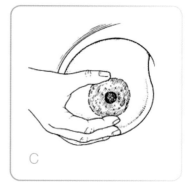
C

5. After massaging your breast, gently roll your nipple between your first finger and thumb (as shown in image C).

6. You can then press and release your breast. Use rhythmic movements. When you press down and release, a small drop of breast milk appears. Do not rub or slide along your nipple as this may hurt.

7. Continue to press and release. After a while, a few drops of breastmilk appears. Collect this in a clean container or syringe.

8. Continue then to press, release and collect.

Using a breast pump

If you're regularly separated from your baby or if there is a delay in breastfeeding after birth, your midwife may recommend using a breast pump to express your milk.

You may also need to use a breast pump if your baby is unable to attach onto your breast. For example, if they were born sick or premature or having challenges attaching to your breast.

How to express using a breast pump

Breast pumps are generally hand-operated or electric (powered by batteries or mains electricity).

Hand-operated pumps work by creating suction when you squeeze the handle or collection container. This may become tiring after a while, so take your time.

Breast pumps may consist of just a collection unit or a two-part collection and storage unit.

Cleaning and sterilising

The collection set and storage container of the breast pump needs to be cleaned after every use.

They should be completely dismantled, washed in hot soapy water and rinsed. Air-dry thoroughly or dry with paper towels. Some manufacturers recommend to sterilise collection and storage containers once a day. Always follow manufacturer's instructions.

What you need

Prepare everything before you start expressing.

You will need:

- a clean collection set
- a clean container for milk storage
- a breast pump
- labels and a pen for labelling containers
- a comfortable chair to sit in while expressing
- a sink with hot running water to wash your hands before putting the pump together
- a facecloth or warm compress to help massage your breasts before expressing
- a small towel to catch any drips
- a drink of water close to hand – you may also want a snack within arm's reach

Give yourself plenty of time and try not to feel rushed.

How to use an electric breast pump

1. Wash and dry your hands.
2. Assemble the pump and connect the tubing (if applicable) to the collection set and container.
3. Make sure that the breast pump pressure is set to the minimum setting.
4. Sit in a comfortable chair with your back supported.
5. Place a warm compress (such as a facecloth or flannel) over the breast and massage for 3 to 5 minutes.
6. Position the funnel of the collection set so that your nipple is in the centre.
7. Hold the funnel so that the pump can create a vacuum but try not to press too firmly into the breast tissue as this can prevent milk flow.
8. Turn on the breast pump.
9. Keep the breast pump pressure at the minimum setting for 2 minutes to help stimulate your milk flow.
10. Gradually increase the pressure on the breast pump to the highest pressure that is comfortable for you (this should never be painful).
11. Continue to express until the flow of milk slows down.
12. Turn off the breast pump and, once the suction is released, remove the funnel of the collection set from your breast.
13. Repeat with the second breast. Sometimes a pump may have double collection sets and containers so you can pump both breasts.
14. When finished, put the lid on the storage container or pour the milk into the storage containers.
15. Label with date and time.
16. Wash and dry the collection set to get it ready for next use. See page 45.

How to use a hand pump

1. Wash and dry your hands.
2. Assemble the pump.
3. Make sure you are in a comfortable position with your back supported.
4. Begin pumping slowly with even pressure.
5. Increase the pressure gradually (this should never be painful).
6. When finished, put the lid on the storage container or pour the milk into a storage container.
7. Label with the date and time.
8. Wash and dry the pump to get it ready for the next use. See page 45.

Storing expressed breast milk

Use a washed container. Any container will do as long as it has an airtight seal and can be washed or sterilised and labelled easily. You may also choose to use disposable one-use breast milk storage bags.

Label each container with date and time. You can keep stored milk:

- sealed outside of the fridge for up to 4 hours in temperatures less than 20 degrees
- in a fridge for up to 5 days (place it at the back of the shelf above the vegetable compartment and not inside the door)
- in the icebox in your fridge for up to 2 weeks
- in a fridge freezer for 3 months
- in a deep freezer for up to 6 months

Heating expressed breast milk

When you are expressing, the breast milk should be chilled or frozen as quickly as possible. Follow these guidelines for defrosting and warming up expressed breast milk.

Defrosting frozen milk

Breast milk can be defrosted in the fridge, normally in around 12 hours. Alternatively, hold the bottle or bag of frozen milk under warm running water (a maximum of 37°C or 99°F).

Don't leave frozen breast milk to defrost at room temperature.

Once fully thawed, previously frozen breast milk may be kept at room temperature for a maximum of 2 hours or in the fridge for up to 24 hours.

Don't thaw or heat frozen breast milk in a microwave or in boiling water. These can damage its nutritional and protective qualities and create hot spots that could scald your baby.

Thawed breast milk left at room temperature should be fed to your baby within 2 hours or thrown away. Never re-freeze breast milk once thawed.

Warming up milk

Healthy full-term babies can drink breast milk at room temperature or warmed to body temperature. Some have a preference, others don't seem to mind.

To warm your milk, place the breast milk bottle or bag into a cup, jug or bowl of lukewarm water for a few minutes to bring it to body temperature (37°C or 99°F). Alternatively, use a bottle warmer. Do not allow the temperature to go above 40°C (104°F).

Do not use a microwave, as this can overheat your milk.

Gently swirl the bottle or bag, without shaking or stirring, to mix any separated fat.

Stopping breastfeeding

You can continue to breastfeed when your baby starts eating solid foods, until your baby is up 2 years of age and beyond. You can stop when it suits you and your child.

If you choose to stop breastfeeding before they start eating solid foods, do it slowly. Speak with your public health nurse, GP, GP practice nurse or go to your local breastfeeding support group for information and support.

How to stop breastfeeding

1. Drop a breastfeed every 2 to 3 days for the first few weeks. Begin with the feeds during the day.
2. Give your child a feed from a cup or bottle during the times you do not offer breast milk.
3. After your child gets used to this new routine, stop another of the daily breastfeeds.
4. Keep doing this feed by feed, until your supply of breast milk has stopped completely.

If your breasts feel hard and uncomfortable at any stage, try hand expressing a little milk (see page 44) – just enough so you feel comfortable.

If you are concerned about your breasts or about stopping breastfeeding, or about your own supply of breast milk, contact your local supports (see above).

Formula-feeding

Talk to your midwife or public health nurse if breastfeeding did not go as planned or you have chosen to formula feed.

There are a number of options available. You can express breast milk, use a combination of formula and breast milk or use formula alone.

Your nurse or midwife will give you information on all these options, including how to safely prepare formula for your baby (see page 50).

Formula milk is also known as formula feed, baby formula or infant formula. Most formula milk is made from cow's milk. It comes in powdered form or in 'ready to feed' cartons.

Like any food, powdered infant formula is not sterile and may contain bacteria. This is why equipment like bottles and teats need to be sterilised (page 50).

Types of formula milk

First infant formula

First infant formula is the type of formula recommended for newborns. This should always be the formula you use and is recommended until your baby is 12 months old.

Hungry baby milk

Hungry baby formula contains more casein than whey. Casein is a protein that is harder for babies to digest.

It's often described as suitable for 'hungrier babies'. There is no evidence that hungry baby milk helps babies settle better.

Follow-on formula

Follow-on formula is sometimes called 'number 2 milk'. Switching to follow-on formula at 6 months has no benefits for your baby.

From 6 months you should begin weaning to solids (see page 59) and aim for a healthy balanced diet. Your baby can carry on having first infant formula as their main drink until they are 12 months old.

Other types of milk

Do not give a baby under the age of 1:

- regular cow's milk as a drink – it can be used when preparing food (see page 60)
- sheep's milk
- goat's milk
- condensed milk
- plant-based milks such as oat, soya, almond or rice milk

Soy formula

Do not use soy formula unless it has been prescribed by your paediatrician or GP.

Bonding during bottle feeds

Feeding is a great chance for you and your baby to get to know each other. Make the most of this bonding time by:

- staying in close contact – consider opening your shirt and doing skin to skin
- looking into your baby's eyes and they will often look back at you – this helps them feel safe and loved
- taking it slowly and enjoying the cuddles
- resisting the urge to multi-task – this is your time with your baby

Always use your arm and hand to bottle feed. Never prop the bottle, for example on a cushion, as it increases the risk of your baby choking. It could also reduce bonding time.

What you need

To prepare formula milk correctly, you will need:

- a clean work surface
- facilities to wash your hands and equipment
- at least 6 bottles, lids and teats
- formula powder
- suitable water (see page 52) and a way to boil it
- a bottle brush and a small teat brush
- sterilising equipment like a steam, chemical or microwave kit
- tongs to help you grip the equipment

If you have a visual impairment, use wide-necked bottles. They are easier to fill.

Sterilising equipment

You must sterilise all feeding equipment until your baby is at least 12 months old.

Incorrect preparation or bad hygiene could make your baby seriously ill.

Cleaning

Clean and sterilise all feeding equipment before you use it. Follow these steps to clean the equipment:

1. Wash your hands well with soap and warm water. Dry your hands with a clean towel.
2. Wash all the feeding equipment in hot soapy water, such as the bottles, teats, lids and tongs.
3. Use a clean bottle brush and teat brush to scrub the inside and outside of the bottles and teats to make sure you remove any leftover milk from the hard-to-reach places.
4. Rinse the bottles and teats well in clean running water.

Types of sterilisers

You can use boiling water, a chemical steriliser or a steam kit to sterilise equipment. A steam steriliser is the best. You can get plug-in or microwaveable sterilisers too.

If using boiling water

Fill a large saucepan with tap water and make sure all equipment is completely covered by the liquid. Make sure there are no trapped air bubbles.

Cover the saucepan and bring it to the boil. Boil for at least three minutes. Make sure the feeding equipment is fully covered with boiling water at all times. Keep the saucepan covered until you need to use the equipment.

Putting bottles together after sterilising

1. Make sure your hands and the work surface are clean.
2. Touching only the outside of the collar, place it over the teat and use sterile tongs to pull the teat through the collar.
3. Screw the collar onto the bottle and tighten fully.
4. Place the cap over the bottle, being sure not to touch the inside of the cap when doing this.
5. Store the bottles in a clean place.

If put together correctly the empty bottles and bottles with sterile water will be safe for 24 hours. If not used within 24 hours, sterilise again. Once you open a bottle to add water or powder it is not sterile.

Keep all sterilising equipment and hot water out of reach of children.

Dishwashers do not sterilise bottles or feeding equipment.

Water supply

Boiled tap water is usually the safest type of water to use. Know the safety of your local water supply.

Your local water supply

Public water supplies and large private group water schemes are regulated by European law and are safe to drink unless you are told otherwise.

If you use water from a private well, you should check that it is safe to drink. See epa.ie for householder information on private wells and information on drinking water on hse.ie.

Using tap or bottled water

Tap water is usually safe to use. But there may be times that you need to use bottled water. For example if:

- you are travelling abroad
- you have a private well and are not sure that the water is safe to drink
- there is a 'boil notice' on your local water supply, or
- you have a water softener system

Water softener system

If you have a water softener which uses salt (ion-exchange softener), only use water that has not been through the softener for making up your baby's bottles.

There should be a single extra tap to your kitchen sink supplying 'unsoftened water' that you can use for drinking, cooking and making up your baby's bottles. If you are not sure which tap to use, it might be safest to use bottled water until you find out.

When using bottled water to make up a bottle feed

Use still water only. Never use fizzy or sparkling water.

It is best not to use bottled water labeled as 'natural mineral water' to make up your baby's feeds as it can have high levels or sodium (salt) and other minerals. If this is the only water available, use it for the shortest time possible. It is important that your baby gets enough to drink.

Bottled water is not sterile. Always boil bottled water to make up formula. Use a kettle or saucepan to get a rolling boil for 1 minute. Cool in the normal way. Do not boil the same water again.

How to make up a formula feed

1. Empty your kettle and fill it with one litre (1l) of freshly drawn cold tap water and boil. Alternatively, boil one litre (1l) of water in a clean saucepan.

2. Leave the boiled water to cool in the kettle or saucepan. Cool it for 30 minutes, but no longer. This will make sure that the water is not too hot, but also that it is no less than 70°C.

3. Clean the work surface well. Wash your hands with soap and warm water and dry them on a clean towel.

4. Read the instructions on the formula's label carefully to find out how much water and powder you need.

5. Pour the correct amount of water into a sterilised bottle. Water that is 70°C is still hot enough to scald, so be careful.

6. Add the exact amount of formula to the boiled water using the clean scoop provided. Reseal the packaging to protect it from germs and moisture.

7. Screw the bottle lid tightly and shake well to mix the contents.

8. To cool the feed quickly, hold the bottle under cold running water or place it in a large bowl of cold water. Make sure that the cold water does not reach above the neck of the bottle.

9. To check the feed is not too hot, shake the bottle and place a drop of liquid on the inside of the wrist – it should feel lukewarm, not hot. Feed your baby.

10. Throw away any feed that your baby has not taken within 2 hours. If your baby is a slow feeder use a fresh feed after 2 hours.

Measuring exact amounts

It is important to measure the formula and water carefully. Too much or too little formula can cause health problems.

For each 30mls (each ounce) of water, you need 1 level scoop of formula powder. This means the powder should not pile up higher than the side of the scoop. Use the scoop in the formula box. Many formula containers have a leveller stick to help. If not, use a clean knife to level the scoop.

For example, if you are making up a 90mls (3 ounce) feed, you will need to add 3 level scoops of formula to 90mls of water that has been boiled and then cooled for 30 minutes.

> ### Automatic formula makers
> The Food Safety Authority of Ireland (FSAI) does not recommend the use of formula preparation machines or automatic machines to prepare bottles of powdered infant formula. There is not enough research to support the safety of these machines.

Preparing feeds in advance

To safely store made-up bottles:

- make up bottles following steps 1 to 8 above
- place cooled bottles in the back of the fridge

- make sure the temperature of the fridge is 5°C or less
- throw away any feed not used within 24 hours – this helps to protect your baby from illness such as gastroenteritis (vomiting and diarrhoea)

Never use a microwave to warm feeds. Microwaves heat unevenly and may cause 'hot spots' that could scald your baby's mouth

How to warm up refrigerated bottle feeds

1. Remove the bottle from the fridge just before you need it.
2. To warm it, place it in a bowl of warm water, making sure the level of the water is below the neck of the bottle. You can also use a bottle-warmer.
3. Do not warm it for more than 15 minutes.
4. Check the temperature of the milk by dripping a little onto the inside of your wrist. It should feel lukewarm, not hot.
5. Throw away any feed that your baby has not taken within two hours. Never re-warm feeds.

How much formula milk to give your baby

If you are bottle-feeding, let your baby decide how much they want. Do not try to make your baby finish a bottle if they do not want to. Never re-use leftover milk once your baby finishes feeding. Throw it away.

Get advice from your GP or public health nurse if your baby is sick and not feeding well.

How much a baby usually drinks

The following table is a guide only. Some babies might drink a little more, other babies might drink a little less. If you have concerns about the amount of formula your baby is taking, contact your public health nurse or GP.

Your baby's age	Average number of feeds in 24 hours	Average daily fluid intake according to baby's weight
Birth to 3 months	6 to 8 (feeding every 3 to 4 hours)	150ml per kg (2½ fluid ozs per lb)
4 to 6 months	4 to 6 (feeding every 4 to 6 hours)	150ml per kg (2½ fluid ozs per lb)

See safefood.eu for more information.

See pages 66 and 67 for advice on milk feeds and other drinks when your baby starts solid foods.

For breastfed and formula-fed babies

Other drinks

Breastfed babies get all the nourishment they need from your milk. They do not need any other drinks.

If you are breastfeeding your baby, do not give them any other drinks unless advised to do so by your GP or public health nurse. Giving them other drinks could reduce the amount of breast milk that they get.

Give your baby breast milk or formula milk as their main drink until they are at least 12 months old. Your baby generally does not need extra drinks.

Cooled boiled water is the most suitable drink if your baby does need extra drinks between feeds.

Advice on drinks for your baby

Don't give your baby:

✗   juice – this includes diluted pure unsweetened fruit juices

✗   cow's milk – it is not suitable for babies under 12 months

✗   tea – it reduces their iron uptake

Don't add any of the following to your baby's bottle:

✗   sugar, rusks or baby rice

✗   any medicines unless advised by your GP or paediatrician.

Do:

✔   Introduce a cup or free flow beaker for drinks of cooled boiled water from about 6 months.

✔   Aim to replace all bottles (if you're using them) with a cup or beaker by the time your baby is about 1 year old.

Vitamin D

Vitamin D helps us to build and maintain strong bones and teeth. It also helps the immune system. Low-levels of vitamin D in children can cause rickets. This is a condition that leads to soft bones.

Vitamin D3 supplements

Our bodies can make vitamin D from the sun. But babies cannot safely get the vitamin D they need from the sun.

You should give your baby 5 micrograms of vitamin D3 as a supplement every day from birth to 12 months if they are:

- breastfed
- taking less than 300mls or 10 fluid oz (ounces) of infant formula a day

Due to a change in EU law (February 2020), there is an increase in the amount of vitamin D3 added to infant formula.

- All babies who are being breastfed should continue to get a vitamin D3 supplement after birth, even if you took vitamin D3 during pregnancy or while breastfeeding.
- You do not need to give your baby a vitamin D3 supplement if they are fed more than 300mls or 10 fluid oz (ounces) of infant formula a day.

There are many suitable infant vitamin D3 supplements available to buy in Ireland. Use a supplement that contains vitamin D only and always check with your pharmacist.

All children aged 1 to 4 years need to take a vitamin D supplement during winter. See page 69.

Buying vitamin D3 supplements

You can buy vitamin D3 supplements for babies in pharmacies and some supermarkets.

Talk to your pharmacist and read the information on the label carefully.

All supplements and medicines should be keep out of children's sight and reach at all times.

Baby wind

Wind is air that your baby has swallowed while feeding, crying or yawning. Babies need help to relieve trapped wind.

Signs of trapped wind

Common signs of trapped wind include squirming or crying during a feed, or looking uncomfortable and in pain if laid down after feeds

How to wind your baby

To wind your baby, hold them upright and gently pat or rub their back.

You can hold them up against your shoulder.

Skin-to-skin contact may relax your baby and they may wind more easily.

Walk with your baby in your arms or in a baby sling. The upright position gently helps to relax them.

Put a gentle little bump or bounce in your walk.

Breastfeeding and wind

Make sure your baby is positioned and attached well to the breast. Ask your public health nurse or lactation consultant to observe a breastfeed if you need help.

Hand expressing a small amount of milk before feeding can help to slow down the flow of milk.

Formula-feeding and wind

Tilt the bottle so the teat and bottle neck are always full of milk. If your baby has a lot of trapped wind, try changing the teat on the bottle.

Reflux

Reflux happens when something in your baby's tummy, like milk, leaks back up into their mouth.

Reflux is different from vomiting, where your baby's muscles forcefully contract.

Reflux is common and can affect up to 40% of babies.

It usually occurs because a baby's food pipe (oesophagus) is still developing. It generally begins around 8 weeks old and improves as your baby gets older.

As your baby gets older, the ring of muscle at the bottom of their oesophagus fully develops. This stops stomach contents leaking out.

Signs and symptoms of reflux

Your baby may not show any signs of reflux or they may show the following:

- spitting up milk during or after feeds
- refusing feeds, gagging or choking
- persistent hiccups or coughing
- excessive crying or crying while feeding

You do not need to be worried about reflux if your baby is feeding well, happy and gaining weight as normal.

When to get medical advice

Contact your public health nurse or GP if reflux starts after 6 months of age or continues beyond 1 year.

You should also get their advice if your baby:

- spits up feeds frequently or refuses feeds
- coughs or gags while feeding
- frequently projectile vomits
- cries a lot or is very irritable
- has green or yellow vomit, or vomits blood
- has blood in their poo or persistent diarrhoea
- has a swollen or tender tummy
- has a high temperature (fever) of 38°C or above
- is not gaining much weight, or is losing weight
- arches their back during or after a feed, or draws their legs up to their tummy after feeding

How to help your baby with reflux

- Wind your baby during feeds (see page 57).
- Hold them upright for a period of time after the feed.

Breastfeeding and reflux

Have your feeding technique, positioning and attachment checked by your public health nurse.

Your lactation consultant and the HSE's online Ask our Breastfeeding Expert services can also give you support and advice. See mychild.ie

Formula feeding and reflux

Talk to your public health nurse to make sure that your baby is taking the correct amount of formula for their age.

To help their symptoms, try:

- offering smaller but more frequent feeds instead of a large volume in one go
- feeding in a more upright position

Weaning your baby to solids

Weaning your baby to solids means starting to feed your baby solid food, instead of just milk.

Introducing your baby to weaning and spoon feeds is an exciting milestone. It's an opportunity for you and your family to share and enjoy food together.

Your baby will be exploring new tastes and textures and they will learn from you. Progress may seem slow. With time and persistence, your baby will develop this important life skill.

When to start

Babies develop at different stages. Begin introducing solids when your baby is ready. This should be around 6 months. This is the same for both breastfed and formula-fed babies.

You should not give your baby solid foods before 17 weeks (4 months) because:

- their kidneys are not mature enough to handle food and drinks other than milk
- their digestive systems are not yet developed enough to cope with solid foods
- breast milk or formula milk is all your baby needs until they are 6 months old
- introducing other foods or fluids can displace the essential nutrients supplied by breast or formula milk
- introducing solids too early can increase the risk of your child having obesity later in life
- it can increase their risk of allergy

Don't wait later than 26 weeks (6 months). This is because:

- your baby's energy needs can no longer be met by either breast milk or formula milk alone
- iron stores from birth are used up by 6 months and their iron needs can no longer be met by milk alone
- it delays their opportunity to learn important skills, including self-feeding
- introducing different textures stimulates the development of muscles involved in speech

Signs your baby is ready

Signs that your baby is ready for solid food include:

- Able to sit up with support and can control their head movements.
- Not fully satisfied after a milk feed.
- Demands feeds more frequently for over a week.
- Shows an interest in food or reaches out for food.
- Watches others with interest when they are eating.
- Chews and dribbles more frequently (this could also be a sign of teething).

Stages of weaning

The weaning process takes place in three stages. It starts with the first spoon feeds at 4 to 6 months.

By 12 months, your baby should be enjoying family meals.

Did you know?

Homemade food is often cheaper, more nutritious and tastier than jars of baby food bought in shops. You can cook a batch and freeze in small batches.

Liquids used to prepare solid food

You can use:

- ✔ breast milk or formula milk
- ✔ water or stock from cooked vegetables
- ✔ cooled boiled water
- ✔ pasteurised full fat cow's milk (small amounts)

Because they contain a lot of salt, do not use:

- ✘ gravy
- ✘ stock cubes
- ✘ jars or packets of sauce

Honey should not be given to babies under 12 months even if it has been cooked. It can contain spores of bacteria that could make your child very ill.

Stage of weaning	What texture the food should be	What your baby will learn
Stage 1 From about 6 months of age	Start with thin purées. They should have a soft and runny consistency. You should increase the thickness as your baby gets used to solid food. See stage 1 weaning foods on page 62.	• Taking foods from a spoon • Moving food from the front to the back of the mouth for swallowing • Managing increasingly thicker purées
Stage 2 Between 6 to 9 months of age	Move to thicker purée and add less liquid to purée. Mash foods with a little liquid. Move to mashed foods with soft lumps. Your baby should also start drinking from a cup or beaker. See stage 2 weaning foods on page 63.	• Moving from thick purées to mashed foods, to foods with soft lumps • Chewing lumps • Beginning to feed themselves with bite-sized soft finger foods using hands and fingers • Drinking from a beaker or cup
Stage 3 Between 9 to 12 months of age	Move to lumpy and chopped family foods. By 12 months, your baby should be eating chopped foods. Offer harder finger foods (more textured). By 12 months, use a non-lidded beaker for all drinks other than breastfeeds. See stage 3 weaning foods on page 64.	• Lumpier textures will help with speech, chewing and increase the variety of your baby's diet in later childhood • Self-feeding bite-sized pieces of food using hands and fingers • Drinking from a cup • Learning to eat with a spoon

Stage 1

Ideas for stage 1 foods

Good options for this stage are:

- puréed well-cooked meat (beef, lamb, pork), poultry (chicken, turkey), puréed and boneless white and oily fish and puréed pulses (peas, beans and lentils)
- vegetables made into purée such as carrot, parsnip, turnip, broccoli, cauliflower, butternut squash and courgette
- fruit made into a purée such as banana, stewed apple, pear, peaches, apricots, plums or melon
- cereals such as baby rice

Result to aim for

Be led by your baby. Some babies might take more than 1 teaspoon at their first spoon feed. Other babies might take a couple of days to get the hang of it.

1. Start with 1 teaspoon of food made into a smooth, thin purée
2. Build up to 6 teaspoons at one time
3. Next, introduce solid food at another mealtime
4. Progress to 2 to 3 meals per day, with 5 to 10 teaspoons at each meal
5. Introduce one new food at a time, every 2 to 3 days

Giving your baby food

Always wash your hands and your baby's hands before you prepare food and feed them.

Organise meal times so that your baby eats with the rest of the family when possible.

Choose a time when you are not rushed and under pressure. Turn off distractions such as the television, computer, tablet and your phone – enjoy this special time with your baby

Safety at meal times

Sitting in a highchair is the safest place for a child to sit. It also helps build good eating habits. Make sure they are strapped in safely.

Children can choke on food if they are walking or running around while eating.

Never leave your child alone while they are eating in case they choke.

Always remove bibs after feeding your child. This is to prevent suffocation and strangulation.

Choosing a high chair

Choose a high chair with foot support so that your baby feels stable and can concentrate on learning to eat. They

A five-point safety harness

should be well-supported and comfortable, and not slide around the chair. Look for a five-point safety harness to prevent falls.

Baby-led weaning

Some parents prefer to use a baby-led approach to weaning. See mychild.ie

How long stage 1 lasts

Babies who start spoon feeds at 6 months will usually move through stage 1 quicker than those who start solids earlier. Start with thin purées initially which should increase in thickness as your baby gets used to solid foods.

Stage 2

Ideas for Stage 2 foods

Include the same food as in stage 1, but now include:

- well-cooked eggs
- porridge and wholegrain breakfast cereals which are low in sugar and salt
- bread, rice and pasta
- cheese (pasteurised)
- yoghurt
- meat, poultry, fish, peas, beans and lentils

Pasteurised cow's milk can be used in small amounts to moisten foods.

Finger foods

Finger foods are an important step in learning to chew. You should offer and encourage your baby with suitable finger foods from 7 months old.

Here are some finger food ideas that can be easily handled and enjoyed by your baby:

- Cooked vegetables such as carrot, parsnip, sweet potato, broccoli.
- Peeled fruit such as pear, banana, peaches, melon, avocado.
- Fingers of buttered toast.
- Bread sticks.
- Plain rice or corn cakes.
- Cheese cut into strips.
- Cooked pasta shapes such as fusilli or penne.
- Sliced or shredded meats.
- Fingers of french toast.
- Slices of omelette.
- Homemade pancakes.
- Potato bread or soda bread.
- Dry cereals.

Corn snack and vegetable puff-type finger foods for babies melt in your baby's mouth so they do not have to chew. You should offer more of the foods above rather than relying on these.

Result to aim for

Be led by your baby, and feed to their appetite. Use these portion sizes as a guide.

- 3 meals a day, each about 2 to 4 tablespoons of food.
- 2 to 3 snacks in between main meals.
- Finger foods.
- Foods should be offered before milk feed.
- Some drinks taken from a cup or beaker.

Stage 3

Ideas for Stage 3 foods

Continue using the same food as stages 1 and 2 and continue to increase the variety in your baby's diet. Most family foods are now suitable without added gravies, sauces, salt or sugar.

> **Snack foods during stage 3 of weaning**
> - A boiled egg and wholemeal toast soldiers.
> - Chopped fruits such as apple or banana.
> - A rice cake.
> - Vegetable sticks such as soft cooked carrot.
> - Yoghurt.
> - Small wholemeal scone with butter.
> - Beans on toast.
> - Home-made soup.
>
> Choose wholegrain bread, brown pasta and rice. These provide more fibre for your baby. For fussy babies or children mix brown and white pasta or rice to begin with.

Result to aim for

Be led by your baby, and feed to their appetite. Use these portion sizes as a guide.

- 3 meals of about 4 to 6 tablespoons.
- 2 to 3 snacks.
- Able to manage more than 2 textures in one meal.
- All drinks (other than breastfeeds) taken from a cup or beaker by 12 months.

Do not give your baby

✗ raw shellfish as this can cause food poisoning

✗ swordfish, shark, marlin or tuna if your child is under 12 months - these fish contain high levels of mercury

✗ honey

✗ unpasteurised cheese, milk or yoghurt

✗ undercooked eggs

✗ sugar

✗ salt, gravies, packets or jars of sauces, packets of soup or meal makers or stock-cubes

✗ tea or coffee

✗ liver

✗ processed or cured meats such as sausages, ham or bacon

Common concerns

Gagging

Gagging is a normal reflex babies have. It happens when your baby is learning how to move lumps of food around their mouth. It is a normal part of learning to eat and swallow.

Gagging is not choking, but it can be scary for parents when it happens. You might feel like you should stop offering lumpier textures to your baby. But your baby will gag less over time if you challenge them with new and different textures.

Gagging is a sign that your baby can protect their airway and is learning to clear food from the back of their mouth. It will happen less when your baby is offered different textures and learns what they need to do to deal with them.

The phase when your baby is gagging regularly will last longer if you keep giving them smooth and lump-free purée. Make sure you move them onto the next stage and through the rest of the stages as recommended.

Foods your child could choke on

Always cut food to a size that your child can chew and eat safely. Grapes, cherry tomatoes and similar-shaped food should be cut into quarters (or smaller) lengthways.

Do not give popcorn, whole nuts, marshmallows or hard sweets to your toddler. These foods should never be given to children under 5 years of age.

Milk feeds and introducing solid foods

Introducing solid foods to your baby will gradually reduce the amount of milk feeds they need.

If your baby is breastfed

There is no need to move from breast milk to formula milk when introducing solid food. You can continue to breastfeed your baby while they are starting solid foods, until they are up to 2 years of age and beyond.

If you have made the decision to stop breastfeeding, see page 48.

If your baby is formula-fed

If you are not breastfeeding, you need to give to your baby a first infant formula (number 1) until they are 12 months old. Once your baby starts on solid foods, the amount of formula that they drink will reduce gradually.

Stage 2 of solid food (6 to 9 months): 3 to 4 feeds about 600mls (21oz) per day

Stage 3 of solid food 9 to 12 months: about 400mls (14oz) per day

Follow-on milks or 'number 2' milks are not necessary or recommended.

Drinks for your baby

Drinks for babies under 6 months

From birth, breast milk or formula milk meets your baby's needs for food and drink to help them grow and develop. They do not need other drinks.

Drinks for babies over 6 months

From 6 months on, offer your baby cooled boiled water in a free-flow beaker at meal or snack times. Boil and cool water before giving it to your baby. You need to keep doing this until they are 12 months old. Both tap and bottled water need to be boiled and then cooled.

You can use small amounts of pasteurised full fat cow's milk to mix in with weaning foods from 6 months onwards. It is not suitable as a drink until your baby is 12 months old.

Drinks for babies over 12 months

You can offer full-fat cow's milk instead of formula as the main milk drink after 12 months.

Drinks that are not suitable for babies

Tea or coffee

Tea and coffee make it difficult for your baby to absorb iron. They also contain caffeine which could affect their sleep.

Fizzy drinks

They have a lot of sugar or acid, which is harmful to teeth. Fizzy drinks also fill up your baby's tummy and they might not want to eat their meals.

Fruit juices

Fruit juices are not recommended. They contain sugar, so can damage your child's teeth. If you choose to offer juices, give only small amounts of well-diluted, unsweetened fruit juice. To do this, dilute 1 measure of pure fruit juice to 8 to 10 measures of cooled boiled water. Use a cup or beaker. Only give this at mealtimes or with snacks.

When to start using a beaker or a cup

Your baby can start drinking from a beaker from 6 months on. You can use it for cooled boiled water, expressed breast milk or formula milk.

Use a lidded beaker that is non-valved with a free-flowing spout. Drinking from a cup or beaker helps your baby to develop their swallow further.

By 12 months of age, your baby should be using a non-lidded beaker for all drinks other than breastfeeds.

A healthy and balanced diet

It's important for your child to have a healthy and balanced diet. This helps their growth and development.

Children's food pyramid

Children aged 1 to 4 years old have small tummies but they have high nutritional needs. They can only eat small amounts. Offer them three meals and two to three snacks every day. All their food needs to be nourishing.

The children's food pyramid sets out how many daily servings your child should have from each food shelf.

Children aged 1 to 2 years need:

- cereals and breads, potatoes, pasta and rice for energy - 3 to 4 servings a day
- vegetables, salad and fruit for vitamins and minerals - 2 to 3 servings a day
- milk, yogurt and cheese for calcium and healthy bones and teeth - 3 servings a day
- meat, poultry, fish, eggs, beans and nuts for protein - 2 servings a day

You can find the children's food pyramid on www.mychild.ie/nutrition

Children aged 1 to 4 should have limited fats, spreads and oils. Too much can be bad for their health.

Examples of a small amount:

- 1 teaspoon of spread on bread
- half teaspoon oil in cooking

Try grilling, baking and steaming instead of frying or roasting with oil or fat.

Your child's daily diet shouldn't have food and drinks high in fat, sugar and salt. They are linked to being overweight in childhood.

These include:

- sweets
- chocolate
- biscuits
- cakes
- fizzy drinks
- crisps

Nutrients

It's important for the growth and development of babies and children that their diet includes key nutrients like:

- iron
- vitamin D
- vitamin C
- omega 3 fats

Vitamin D is important for healthy bones. Your child can get it from:

- oily fish – herring, mackerel, salmon, trout, sardines
- eggs
- 'fortified' cereals and milks that have added vitamin D

Vitamin D supplements

Some babies under 12 months need a vitamin D supplement each day. See page 56.

All children aged 1 to 4 years need to take a vitamin D supplement during winter. Give them 5 micrograms of a vitamin D3-only supplement from Halloween (October 31st) to St Patrick's Day (March 17th). Liquid drops are usually best for this age group.

Iron

Iron is important in your child's diet. It helps them grow. Iron also helps make new red blood cells that carry oxygen from your child's lungs to their body.

Babies are born with stores of iron that last about six months. From 6 months, your growing child needs to get iron from the foods that they eat.

The best sources of iron

Meats such as beef, lamb, pork and poultry contain iron. Red meat is the best source of iron. You should give it to your child three or four times a week. Liver is not recommended as it contains too much vitamin A for babies.

Other good sources of iron include eggs (well-cooked), lentils, green leafy vegetables such as spinach or broccoli and fortified breakfast cereals (make sure they are low in salt and sugar). Check the cereal box label for ones that contain at least 12mg of iron per 100g.

Vitamin C can help your child's body to absorb non-meat sources of iron. They can get it from some:

* fresh fruits – oranges, mandarins, berries or kiwi fruit
* fresh vegetables – broccoli, cauliflower and peppers

For example, add some chopped berries to a breakfast porridge or cereal that contains iron.

Anaemia

Your child may develop a condition called anaemia if they do not get enough iron in their diet. Anaemia happens when you don't have enough healthy red blood cells to carry adequate oxygen around the body. If your child has anaemia, they might seem:

* tired and pale with a poor appetite
* less able to fight infection

Contact your public health nurse or GP if you are concerned that your child may have anaemia.

Omega 3

Omega 3 fats are important for brain and eye development. You can get omega 3 from oily fish such as salmon, mackerel, herring, trout and sardines. It is recommended to include two 1oz portions of oily fish a week from 7 months of age. Offer your child (aged 1 to 4 years) oily fish once a week.

Milk and nut milks

From 12 months, your child should not drink more than 600mls of full fat cow's milk per day. This includes the milk used on their breakfast cereal. Your child should drink milk from a cup or beaker, unless you are breastfeeding.

From 12 months, infant formula, follow-on milk or toddler milks are not necessary or recommended.

Do not give your child under 2 years:

- low-fat milk
- dairy alternatives such as almond milk, coconut milk, oat milk. Rice milk is not suitable for children under 4 and a half years old.
- tea or coffee
- fruit juice drinks
- fizzy drinks
- dilutable squashes

Gluten

There is no need to avoid gluten when introducing foods into your baby's diet. You can introduce foods containing gluten any time between 4 months (17 weeks) and 12 months of age.

Give small amounts at first and make sure it is the right consistency (thickness and texture) for their age. See page 59 for information on weaning to solid foods.

Foods containing gluten include bread, pasta, crackers and breakfast cereals.

Food allergies

Recent research shows that you can prevent your child from becoming allergic to certain foods like eggs, milk and peanut if you introduce these foods into your child's diet early (around 6 months).

Foods that can commonly cause allergies include nuts, milk, eggs and fish. You should introduce these foods one at a time. This is because if your baby does have a reaction to a food, you will know what food caused the reaction.

Peanuts

If your baby is 6 months old, do not delay the introduction of peanut into their diet. Use smooth peanut butter or spread that is sugar-free and salt-free.

Talk to your GP or public health nurse first if your baby has bad eczema.

Don't give whole nuts like peanuts to your child until they over the age of 5, as they could cause them to choke.

Other nuts

It is safe to give other nuts like cashews and hazelnuts to your baby in smooth butters or spreads. These must be sugar-free and salt-free.

Dairy

Introduce pasteurised dairy products like cheese (for example cheddar) and yoghurt (natural yoghurt with some fruit puree or chopped fruit) from 6 months.

Cow's milk can be used to prepare solids foods but should not be given to your child as a drink until they are 12 months old. See page 70.

Eggs

You should give well-cooked eggs from 6 months in the right texture and consistency for their stage.

Fish

Fish can be given to your baby when you are introducing solid foods (see page 59). Oily fish (for example salmon, mackerel, sardines and trout) contains omega 3 fats which are essential for brain and eye development. See page 70 for recommended amounts.

Meal planning

Take time to plan your meals in advance. This will help you to introduce variety, eat more nutritious foods, save money and rely less on convenience and processed foods.

Cook just one main meal for the whole family. Try to make this meal healthy and balanced including foods from the food pyramid shelves (see page 68).

Fussy or picky eating

Fussy, faddy and picky eating is a phase when your child doesn't eat well or refuses to eat certain foods. It is a normal part of their development and can happen around 18 months old. Children's appetites differ greatly.

What to do

Don't be upset if they refuse to eat well the odd day. This is a part of growing up but it can be worrying for parents. If fussy eating continues, ask your public health nurse, GP or GP practice nurse for advice.

Causes of fussy eating

Your child may be:

- unwell now or recovering from a recent illness
- eating too many snacks between meals
- drinking too much milk or other drinks
- showing their independence

Tips to help fussy eating habits

Your child's relationship with food will develop by watching and learning from what is going on around them. Sit down as a family to enjoy mealtimes.

To help your child to eat well:

- have a daily routine with regular mealtimes where you sit down at a table with your child to eat
- eat lots of different foods in front of your child - they will be more likely to do the same
- involve them in the meals - for example, when you are planning, shopping, preparing, cooking and tidying-up
- offer a wide variety of foods and include their favourite healthy foods regularly
- give small portions on a plate
- let them eat their food first before you give them their drink
- give them enough time to eat
- allow them to stop eating when they say that they are full - wait until the next snack or meal time before offering more food
- be firm but do not force them to eat
- limit distractions – turn off the television, computer, tablet and put your phone away
- try not to rely on food to reward your child for good behaviour or as a comfort if your child is upset. Think of alternatives like stickers or a trip to the playground
- make positive comments about food - avoid placing too much focus on certain foods, like vegetables

Finish the meal after about 30 minutes and accept that is all your child is going to eat. Take away uneaten food without comment. Ignore the fussy behaviour, lots of attention may make them keep it up.

Calm and consistent

Remain calm and continue to approach your child's refusal to eat in a positive way. If your child is active and gaining weight, they are getting enough to eat.

Did you know?

It can take up to 10 to 15 tries before your child will accept a new food.

Sleeping

Sleep is one of the most challenging parts of caring for your child. Your child is going to learn how to settle themselves to sleep and will develop a routine in time. This will take time, but you will get there.

Sleep for newborns

Newborn babies are too young to follow strict routines. Some babies sleep for long periods, others for a short period. See page 75 for information on how much sleep newborn babies need. You can begin a bedtime routine when your baby is between 3 and 6 months (see page 76).

The first few weeks

Your baby's sleep pattern is probably not going to fit in with your sleep pattern. Try to sleep when your baby sleeps.

The first few weeks can be a difficult. It can be frustrating. It will take time to adjust.

Sleeping position

To reduce the risk of cot death (sudden infant death syndrome):

- Always put your baby down to sleep (day and night) on their back.
- Their feet should be at the foot of the cot, crib or Moses basket.
- Keep their head and face uncovered.

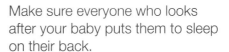
Make sure everyone who looks after your baby puts them to sleep on their back.

Where to put the cot, crib or Moses basket

- Your baby should sleep in their own cot, Moses basket or crib in the same room as you for at least the first six months.
- Do not place the cot, Moses basket or crib near a radiator or heater as it may be too hot.
- Place the cot, Moses basket or crib away from open windows to avoid draughts.

Make it a safe place to sleep

- Do not use cot bumpers (padding around the sides of the cot) as these can increase the risk of suffocation.
- Keep the cot, Moses basket or crib clear of items including pillows, cushions and toys.
- Do not hang ribbons or toys with strings from your baby's cot, Moses basket or crib – your baby could choke on them or be strangled.

See page 202 for more information on how to reduce the risk of cot death (sudden infant death syndrome).

Moving their head

If your baby always lies with their head in the same position, they might develop a 'flat head'. This is known as plagiocephaly.

You can prevent this when putting your baby down to sleep. Turn their head so that sometimes they face left and sometimes they face right.

This will also help your baby's head and neck muscles to develop strength equally on both sides.

Their own room

From 6 months you can move your baby into their own room to sleep, if you have the space. Most young children stay in a cot until they are between 2 and 3 years old.

Change to a low bed to prevent injuries if your child:

- learns to climb out of the cot, or
- grows too big for the cot

Finding their position

At around 6 months your baby will move about during sleep and change their position in the cot. They will find their own sleep position.

Continue to put them down to sleep on their back to reduce the risk of cot death. Check on them while they are asleep to see if they have kicked the blankets over their head or off their body.

Light and noise

The bedroom should be dark. You can keep a night light switched on for older babies and toddlers. See page 78. Use blackout blinds if needed. See page 194 for advice on blind cords.

The room should be as quiet as possible, though you should not worry about a normal level of background noise. Avoid music, mobiles or light-up and electronic toys in or near the cot. These are props. A prop is a physical item your child relies on to go to sleep. They might also disrupt sleep during the night.

If you have a mobile above the cot, phase it out when your baby is five months old.

How much sleep your child needs

Your child's age	Their sleep
From birth to 3 months	Your baby needs about 9 to 18 hours of sleep over a day (an average of 14 and a half hours) – some babies sleep more than others.
	They may go straight to sleep after a feed.
	When possible, put your baby to bed drowsy but awake, so that they wake up where they fall asleep. This might help them to go back to sleep if they wake up during the night.
	Background noises such as music or children playing may not wake them but a sudden loud noise might.
	Limit your caffeine intake if you are breastfeeding (see page 37). This is because caffeine is a stimulant and may keep your baby awake.
3 to 6 months	Your baby needs about 12 to 14 hours sleep over a day. They will usually nap for around 3 to 4 hours.
	They may still go straight to sleep after a feed and then wake for a while before the next feed is due. By about 6 months, your baby will stay awake and be more alert between feeds.
	At this stage, they are starting to identify the difference between day and night. A bedtime routine (see page 76) at this age helps to show your baby that sleep time is approaching.
	It is normal for your baby to wake briefly during the night (see page 79). You should avoid stimulating your baby if this happens, for example by talking loudly or playing with them.

Your child's age	Their sleep
By about 6 months	Your baby needs about 10 to 11 hours of sleep a night. Two to three naps during the day, each for about an hour and a half or 2 hours, is enough.
	They will be less likely to sleep during a feed.
By about 1 year	Your toddler needs about 10 to 12 hours of sleep a night. They won't have a nutritional need for night feeds if they are fully established on solid foods (see page 61).
	Your child might want to feed for comfort or to help them fall back asleep. Some parents may choose to continue feeding at night. For others, it can disturb their sleep. See page 80 for advice on phasing out night feeds.
	They may have 2 naps during the daytime of about one and a half to two hours each. Your toddler should be awake by 3.30pm after their nap. If they sleep later than this, it can interrupt their night-time sleep.
By about 18 months	Your toddler needs about 11 to 12 hours of sleep a night.
	They may have one nap during the daytime of about one and a half to two hours.
By about 2 years	Your toddler needs about 11 to 12 hours of sleep a night.
	They may have one nap during the day of about one a half hours or two and a quarter hours.
	Try not to let your child nap beyond the mid-afternoon. This will help them to be tired and ready for sleep again by night time.

Bedtime routine

Getting your baby to sleep

A bedtime routine is important. You can start this between 3 to 6 months. Build a routine around the last feed before you settle your baby down to sleep.

Have about half an hour between the last feed and your baby settling to sleep. This is to avoid your baby linking feeding to going to sleep.

You can build a routine by:

- making a clear difference between day and night – for example, use dim lights and a low voice in the evening along with relaxing activities like a bath
- encouraging your child to be out in the daylight early in the day and to be active in the evenings. This helps your child to make the hormone melatonin that helps them to go sleep
- having 'wind down' time in the hour before bed
- putting your baby to sleep in the same place when at home
- feeding your baby after a bath or after you change them into sleeping clothes
- avoiding rocking to sleep – they may need to be rocked to get back to sleep if they wake during the night

During the night

- Use a dim light when you feed your baby at night as a bright one may over-stimulate them - yellow or red light is best and avoid blue light.
- Speak to your baby in a quiet calm voice when you are feeding them at night – talking loudly may encourage them to stay awake.
- Put your baby back into the cot drowsy but awake so that they wake up where they fall asleep.
- Don't change your baby's nappy during sleep time unless it is dirty.

Getting your toddler to sleep

Your toddler will thrive when there is a regular bedtime routine. Your toddler should go to sleep and get up around the same time each day.

Make going to bed as predictable as possible. Whenever you can, share bedtimes and storytelling between parents. Create an atmosphere that will help your toddler to sleep:

Before they go to bed

Avoid exciting activities such as playing outside and running around just before bedtime. Do not give them a very large meal or sugary snacks or drinks just before bedtime.

Give them a supper of carbohydrates like bread, rice or cereals and some milk, which helps to produce the sleepy hormone melatonin.

Turn off all screens and the television an hour before bed.

Bed time

Brush their teeth and make sure they have a clean nappy when they go to bed.

You can switch on a night light in the room so that they do not feel upset if they wake up in the dark. The light should be out of their sight. Yellow and red night lights are best. This will give you some light to check on your child during the night. Keep the night light on throughout the night. Your child might get upset if they wake up in the night and it's switched off.

Put them to bed drowsy but awake, so they wake up where they went to sleep.

Read a short bedtime story to help them relax before sleep.

When you leave the room

Leave the bedroom door open so that they can hear some soothing and familiar noises outside.

Comfort toys

Some children like to bring a favourite toy or blanket with them as they settle down to sleep. Make sure it is clean and not a danger to them while they are sleeping. Comfort toys like blankets or teddies allow your child to self-soothe. They are unlikely to disturb their sleep.

Avoid toys with music or lights. This includes mobiles above their cot or bed. If you have a mobile above the cot, phase it out when your baby is five months. It can become something they rely on to fall asleep. It can also stimulate your baby to be more awake.

If you are worried

Every baby and toddler has different sleep patterns. Contact your public health nurse, GP or GP practice nurse for information and advice if you are worried that:

- your baby is not sleeping, or
- their sleep pattern is disturbed
- you are finding it difficult to cope

Waking during the night

Waking up during the night is sometimes called 'night wakening'. It mostly happens to babies and toddlers.

Research shows disturbed sleep at night is one of the most common problems parents have. In Ireland, 30% of mothers with 9-month-old babies said sleep patterns were a problem. 22% of mothers of children aged 3 years continued to identify sleep as a problem.

How children fall asleep at night

Small children usually fall into a deep sleep within 5 minutes of going to sleep. The first two sleep cycles last about three to four hours and are mostly deep sleep.

As your child moves to lighter sleep, they stir and move around. They may open their eyes.

If everything is the same as when they first went to sleep, they will fall asleep again quickly.

But if something is missing, then your child may cry for you. They will want to recreate the same situation they had when they fell asleep. For example, you might have rocked them to sleep at bedtime. They will want you to do this again each time they wake up during the night.

For some parents, it isn't a problem to repeat this. For others, the disruption to their sleep can be very difficult. There are ways you can help your child to learn how to fall asleep again without you being there.

Learning to fall asleep

Your child falling asleep by themselves is a learned behaviour. There are ways you can support this from 6 months of age.

Try to:

- place your child to sleep in their own cot
- avoid 'props' in or near the cot – these include musical or light-up toys and ceiling-hung mobiles
- avoid sleep associations – this may be physical contact with a parent as a child is falling to sleep. For example, rubbing their back, rocking or feeding to sleep. Sleep associations usually develop between 6 and 12 months

When possible, put your baby to bed drowsy but awake, so that they wake up where they fall asleep. Follow the bedtime routine tips on page 77 to 78. There is advice on how to help your child to sleep through the night on page 80.

Helping your toddler to be comfortable falling asleep by themselves is a great skill. Good sleep patterns in childhood can be good for your health as an adult.

Feeding during the night

Young babies will need to feed during the night. They may fall asleep during the feed.

Introducing solid foods begins around 6 months (see page 59). Once your baby is fully established on to solid foods, they will get all the food they need during the day. You can then phase out night feeds. Some parents may choose to continue to breastfeed during the night for other reasons, such as comfort.

How to gradually reduce and stop night feeds:

- decrease the frequency and volume of feeds for bottle-fed babies
- space out the timing of breastfeeding for breastfed babies

If possible, try to avoid your baby falling asleep while feeding. This can lead to them associating or linking sleep with feeding. They may need a feed to go back to sleep if they wake during the night.

Talk to a public health nurse if you have questions about sleep and feeding. If you are breastfeeding, you can also get advice from the 'Ask our breastfeeding expert' service on mychild.ie.

Helping your child sleep through the night

Babies start to sleep for longer periods at night from about 3 months on. You may want to establish a bedtime routine which is done in the same way at roughly the same time each night. This is to help them sleep through the night and begin to know the difference between day and night. A change in routine will take a little time.

Gradual retreat

Some parents feel that not being present when a young child falls asleep is too difficult for them and their child. You can try the 'gradual retreat' technique. It gently teaches your child to fall asleep on their own while you are in the room.

1. Put your child into the cot or bed while they are awake and sit on a chair next to them.
2. Stay there until your child falls asleep.
3. Once your child can consistently fall asleep this way, sit farther and farther away every 3 to 4 nights – eventually you will be out of sight in the hallway.

Some parents find it easier to pretend that they are asleep rather than sitting in a chair.

Be consistent

It is important to be consistent in applying your new routine and not to give up. The first few nights are likely to be very challenging. Often the second or third night is worse than the first night.

But within a few nights to a week, you will begin to see improvement. Make sure to use the bedtime routine tips outlined on page 76 too.

If your toddler wakes up crying every night

Crying is a form of communication and your toddler is telling you something. They may simply be tired.

Make sure they are not hungry by giving them supper as part of their bedtime routine. Change their nappy before they go to bed. Brief awakenings are normal during the night.

Wait a minute or two before checking on your toddler if they wake or cry, as they may fall back to sleep.

If they do not go back to sleep:

1. Settle and soothe them - comfort them and talk softly.
2. Put your child back to sleep in their own cot or bed.
3. When you have resettled your child, don't stay in the room.
4. If they wake and cry again, repeat the steps above.

Teething, illness and a dirty nappy can also cause your child to wake up. Follow the steps above after dealing with the situation. For example, after giving your child liquid paracetamol or changing their nappy.

Toddlers do not normally need to be fed during the night if they are eating a normal family diet (see page 80). Some parents may choose to breastfeed at night for comfort.

Try not to play with them or let them get into your bed. In this way, you are helping them learn that night time is for sleeping. The aim is to let your toddler know that you are there but support them to self-soothe to sleep.

Reward your child with praise for their efforts the next day. Be specific, for example, "you are such a good boy for staying in your bed."

This way of changing your toddler's sleep pattern is gradual. It may take a week or two to work.

Contact your public health nurse or GP for advice if:

- these techniques do not work for you
- lack of sleep is getting you down

Daytime naps

Naps are essential during the day to prevent your child from becoming overtired. If a child is overtired, it can affect their night time sleep.

Some parents say that their children 'never nap'. Usually their child is having short naps in the car or in the buggy.

Generally, a child does not need to nap for more than two hours. Napping habits can differ between children.

Common difficulties with napping

Hidden naps may happen in the car or when you are out walking with your child in a buggy. The timing of these naps can impact on their overall quality of sleep.

Another difficulty can be too little napping during the day and too much sleep at night. If your child is content during the day, then this is not a problem. If they are cranky and out of sorts, then you may wish to wake them earlier in the morning.

Crying

Before they learn to speak, crying is your baby's way of telling you that they need something.

Dealing with crying is one of the hardest parts of parenting. The way you respond to your baby's crying is very important. If you respond calmly, this helps them to manage their distress and feel secure. It also helps to build your relationship.

Give yourself time

Accept offers of help and support from family and friends as this can be a difficult time for you. In the early stages it's not always obvious why your baby is crying or distressed. It takes time to learn to read your baby's signals.

Why your baby might be crying

Babies normally have at least one period of being unsettled each day. They cry for many reasons.

Some reasons for crying include:

- hunger or thirst
- being overfull
- a wet or dirty nappy
- pain from wind (page 57), colic (page 84) or reflux (page 58)
- being too hot or too cold
- being overtired or overstimulated
- loneliness or boredom, or
- being unwell

It can take time to learn what your baby is trying to communicate. Try to be patient with yourself as you get to know your baby.

Dealing with crying

It might be very difficult to remain calm while your baby is crying. Staying calm and using a soothing voice will help your baby to become calm.

Your baby will learn early on that you are able to manage their feelings. This in turn will help them to manage theirs.

You can also soothe your baby by:

- holding them close and moving gently
- feeding
- nappy changing
- rocking your baby gently
- singing to your baby gently or listening to music together
- gently talking to your baby — babies enjoy the soothing sound of their parents' voices, especially when the voice is close and softly spoken
- massaging your baby gently with unscented oil
- placing them safely in a sling (see page 88)
- going for a short walk or drive in the car with your baby
- leaving their nappy off and letting them kick their legs
- giving them a bath (see page 88)

Contact your GP if:

- the crying continues
- the crying sounds unusual, or
- you are worried that your baby is ill

Self-soothing

As your baby gets older, they may be able to calm and soothe themselves. They do this by:

- bringing their hand to their mouth to suck it
- touching and stroking their hands and feet
- making eye contact and touching you

If you are finding it difficult

If you are finding it hard to stay calm or to cope with your baby's crying, then:

- Put your baby down in their cot and go into another room for a moment to calm down.
- Ask someone to come and help you care for your baby while you take a break.
- Contact a relative, friend, your GP or your public health nurse for advice and help.
- Call Parentline for support and advice on 1890 927 277.

Many parents find caring for a baby exhausting, especially if the baby is hard to console. Try and remember this stage will pass. Get support from family, friends and professionals to help you through this time.

Never shake your baby, as this can damage your baby's brain and put them in serious danger.

Colic

Colic is the name for excessive and frequent crying in a baby who is otherwise healthy. Colic is very common and affects 1 in 5 babies.

Colic can be very upsetting for parents. It is hard to see your baby crying so intensely, and it can seem like your baby is in pain.

When colic starts

Colic usually starts when babies are about 2 weeks old. It usually ends by the time they are 4 months old but sometimes it lasts until they are 6 months old.

It is more common in the evening time. Sometimes a baby with colic can cry for many hours during the day or night.

Signs of colic

A baby has colic if they cry:

- for more than 3 hours a day
- for more than 3 days a week, and
- for more than 3 weeks

Babies with colic often have the following symptoms:

- periods of crying where they are harder to console than usual
- restlessness
- drawing their legs up, or arching their backs, or clenching their fists
- going red in the face
- seeming to settle and then having another spell of crying

Babies with colic are fine between periods of crying. Your baby should be feeding well and gaining weight even if they have colic.

Causes of colic

It is not known why some babies get colic. Colic is more common in premature babies. It can be more common if the baby is in a home where somebody smokes.

For a minority of babies, the cause of their colic is intolerance to cow's milk.

How to help your baby with colic

There is no treatment for colic. Different things will help different babies. As you get to know your baby, you will learn what works for you.

Continue breastfeeding on demand or offering your baby formula feeds.

Things that might help:

- Hold your baby close during a crying episode – you are not 'spoiling' your baby by responding to their needs in this way.
- Sit your baby upright during feeds.
- Wind or burp your baby after feeds.
- Gently rock your baby.
- A warm bath.
- Gently massaging your baby's tummy.

There are some other things you may like to try. There is no scientific research to support their use, but some parents find them helpful.

- Movement and motion, for example a walk in the buggy or pram, or a car journey.
- Music.
- 'White noise' like the low frequency noise of a vacuum cleaner, a radio not tuned in properly or 'white noise' music or apps.

Medication

If simple things don't work, talk to your pharmacist or public health nurse about medications that you can get over the counter.

Some parents find drops that can be added to the baby's breast milk or bottle milk are helpful. But there is no scientific evidence that they work.

Formula

Always talk to your public health nurse before changing your baby's formula milk.

Complementary therapies

Be careful about using complementary therapies like herbal remedies. These have not been proven to work and some have been shown to cause serious side effects.

There is no evidence that cranial osteopathy or spinal manipulation work. This manipulates or moves your baby's muscles in a particular way. These could be harmful to your baby.

When you should see your GP

Bring your baby to the GP if:

- you are not sure if your baby has colic or why they are crying
- they are vomiting green stuff (bile)
- they have projectile vomiting
- they have bloody poo
- they are not feeding well
- their symptoms started after you introduced formula
- they are losing weight or not gaining weight
- they have a temperature greater than 38°C

You can also go to the GP if you are concerned or you are finding it hard to cope.

Looking after yourself

Many babies get colic. This is not your fault. You are not spoiling your baby by responding and your baby is not rejecting you.

It can be upsetting when it is difficult to comfort your baby. It can be also upsetting when someone else manages to soothe a baby that has been crying with you for hours.

Remember:

- This will stop eventually – all babies with colic have improved by 4 to 6 months.
- You need to get rest and look after your own wellbeing – if possible ask family and friends for support.

Caring for your child

Getting confident about everyday care and tasks is an important step in your new role as a parent. With time and practice, this gets easier and quicker to do.

Equipment

A correctly-fitted rear-facing car seat is essential when going for drives with your baby. See page 205.

Other useful equipment for moving about with your baby includes:

- a pram or a buggy that can lie back (recline)
- a baby sling

Prams or pushchairs

Pushchairs and strollers are only suitable for newborns if they recline fully. This means your baby can lie down.

Check to see if:

- it is sturdy
- has brakes that work
- the folding mechanisms are securely locked into place
- complies with European safety standards
- has a five-point harness — that's a harness with five straps that are all properly secured to provide really effective restraint

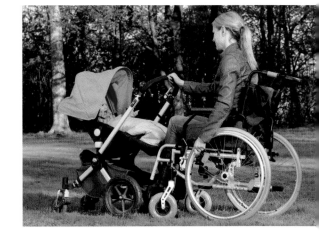

When you're out and about

- Do not use pillows or cushions as they could cause suffocation.
- Hold onto the buggy or pram securely to prevent it slipping from your grasp.
- Always put wheel brakes on when you stop, even on a flat surface.
- Do not hang bags on the handle of the pram or buggy as this may cause it to tip over. Place them in the basket underneath.
- Do not attach your dog's lead to your buggy – they could pull the buggy away.
- If your baby falls asleep in a seated position, always place them on their back as soon as possible.

Sling safety

Always follow **TICKS** guidelines:

- **T**ight
- **I**n view at all times
- **C**lose enough to kiss
- **K**eep chin off chest
- **S**upported back

Practice putting slings and baby carriers on and taking them off before using them with your baby.

Baby carriers and slings can be a suffocation risk unless you use them correctly. Make sure that your baby or toddler is upright, their head is supported and they do not get too hot. Always follow the TICKS guidance (see picture).

If your baby falls asleep, remove them from the sling or carrier as soon as possible. Place them on their back on a flat surface.

Do not drink or make hot drinks or cook while holding your baby in your arms or in a sling. Your baby could be scalded.

Take care not to trip or fall when going up or down stairs or walking on uneven ground.

Contact your GP or paediatrician before using a sling or babywearing coat if your baby:

- is younger than four months of age
- had a low birth weight
- was premature
- has a medical condition, including respiratory conditions and colds

Bathing your baby

Bath time is a chance for you and your baby to have fun, play and interact. A bath two or three times a week is enough to keep your baby clean.

Preparing for the bath

Have everything you need ready before you start:

- a baby bath or basin
- a clean nappy
- clean clothes
- two towels
- some cotton wool

Use plain water and no liquid soaps for babies under 1 month.

Other tips:

- Plan the bath for a quiet time of the day.
- Choose a time when your baby is not too hungry or tired. Do not bathe them just after a feed.
- Have everything you need within easy reach so you don't need to turn away from your baby while they are in the bath.
- Close windows to prevent a draught.
- Make sure the room is warm as babies can get cold quickly.

Water temperature

Your baby's skin needs cooler water than your own. Water that may feel barely warm to you could be painfully hot for your baby.

Follow these steps to get the correct temperature:

1. Put the cold water in the bath or basin first.
2. Then put the warm water in.
3. If your bath has a single tap with a hot and cold feed, make sure you run the cold water again to cool the taps so they won't burn your baby.
4. The water level should be just high enough to cover your baby's tummy when they are lying down.
5. Mix the water well to ensure there are no 'hot spots'.
6. Always check the temperature of the bathwater with your elbow – your hands are not heat-sensitive enough.
7. If using a bath thermometer, make sure the temperature is around 36°C.

How to bathe your baby

1. Hold your baby on your knee and clean their face.
2. Hold their head over the basin, bath, baby bath or sink and wash their hair.
3. Make sure you dry their head.
4. Slip off their nappy and wipe their bottom.

5. Get ready to lower your baby into the basin, bath, baby bath or sink. Have one of your arms behind their shoulders and neck, holding their outside arm with your hand.

6. Place your other hand under their bottom.

7. Lower your baby slowly into the water so they don't feel as though they are falling.

8. When their bottom is resting on the floor of the basin, bath, baby bath or sink, you can remove that hand to wash them.

9. Use your other hand to keep your baby's head out of the water.

10. When finished, put the hand you used to wash them back under their bottom.

11. Hold their legs with that arm as they will be slippery. Then lift them out onto the towel.

12. Pat them dry. Don't forget to dry their skin folds and creases.

13. Empty the basin, bath, baby bath or sink.

Now is a good time to try baby massage, this can help soothe them. Don't use any oils on their skin for the first month.

Bath safety

✗ Never leave your baby alone in the bath, not even for a second as they are at risk of scalds and drowning.

✗ Do not use bath seats – your baby could slip out or tip forwards or sideways into the water.

✗ Do not rely on a toddler or older child to mind your baby in the bath.

✗ Do not leave babies, toddlers or young children in the bathroom without adult supervision.

Keeping your baby clean between baths

A 'top and tail' wash is a quick way to keep your baby clean between baths.

Use pieces of cotton wool and a bowl of warm water. Wet each piece of cotton wool in the bowl and then squeeze it out so it is just damp when you use it.

Use different pieces of cotton wool to clean:

- your baby's face and hands
- the folds or creases under the neck
- the folds and creases under arms
- the nappy area

Your baby's fingernails

Your baby's nails are very soft in the first few weeks after birth. You could easily cut their skin when you cut the nails. You may find it better to gently peel the nails off or use an emery board to file them.

After a week or two, buy special baby nail clippers or small round-ended safety nail scissors from a pharmacy.

Wait until your baby is relaxed or asleep before trying to cut nails. Ask someone else to help you if you need to.

Taking care of your baby's umbilical cord

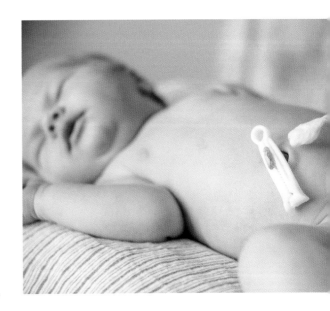

The umbilical cord stump should fall off between 5 to 15 days after birth.

Before the umbilical cord stump falls off:

- Wash your hands before and after you touch the cord.
- Clean around the base of the cord if needed with cotton wool and cooled boiled water.
- Keep the belly button area dry after you clean it.
- Check the umbilical cord at every nappy change to make sure there is no redness there.
- Fold your baby's nappy down, away from the cord.

After the stump falls off

The umbilical stump will dry out, turn black and drop off. After the stump comes off, it usually takes about seven to 10 days for the belly button to heal completely.

Ask your midwife or public health nurse for advice if you see any bleeding or discharge from your baby's belly button.

Go to your GP if you see redness on the skin of your baby's stomach around the stump, or there is a foul smell.

Nappies

Newborn nappies

A newborn's poos are sticky and green or black in colour for the first few days. This is called meconium. This will change later to a yellow colour.

Day	Wet nappies	Dirty nappies
Day 1 to 3	At least 1 to 2	At least 1 to 2 black or dark green poos
Day 3 to 5	At least 3, heavier	At least 3 yellow poos
Day 5	At least 5, heavy	At least 3 large soft and seedy yellow nappies

How many nappies

Most babies have:

- at least 6 wet nappies each day
- at least 1 dirty nappy each day – some breastfed babies may have more or less than this

Some babies have a dirty nappy at every feed and others have a dirty nappy once a day. Your baby might not have a dirty nappy for one to two days. If the poo is soft when they have a dirty nappy, your baby is not constipated. You will soon see a pattern for your baby.

Contact your public health nurse, GP or lactation consultant if you have any concerns.

Smell and texture

Breastfed babies usually have runny poos that do not smell. Formula-fed babies have poos that are usually more formed and smellier.

If you have recently introduced formula, changed formula or introduced solids, then expect a change in texture, colour and smell. Pain relief and other medication will also cause changes.

Nappy changing

Bonding time

Chat with your baby or toddler while changing their nappy. It makes the experience more pleasant for both of you.

What you need

You will need:

- a bowl filled with warm water
- a clean nappy
- clean clothes
- towels
- some cotton wool
- nappy disposal bag

Plain water

Plain water (with no soap or detergent) is best for the first month. Always check water temperature with your elbow.

Wipes

If using wipes, make sure they are fragrance-free and alcohol-free.

How to change a nappy

1. Get everything ready before you begin.
2. If you are using a changing table, make sure everything you need is within reach.
3. Wash your hands before removing the nappy.
4. Clean your baby's genitals and bottom with cotton wool and water or an unscented wipe.
5. Gently lift your baby's legs by holding their ankles. This allows you to clean underneath.
6. For girls and boys, always wipe from front to back.
7. For a baby boy, there is no need to retract the foreskin. Point his penis downwards before replacing the nappy.
8. Let the area dry. There is no need to use powders.
9. Slide a new and open nappy under your baby by gently lifting their legs at the ankles. The new nappy should be snug but not tight.
10. Wash your hands after changing the nappy.

Safe nappy changing

Falls

Never leave your baby alone on a raised surface, even for a few seconds. Babies can roll off changing tables, beds and other raised surfaces. These falls can result in serious head injuries.

Suffocation

Nappy disposal bags and sacks and other plastic bags are a suffocation risk. The flimsy material of a nappy sack can cling to your baby's face causing suffocation.

Do not store nappy sacks or any other plastic material within your baby's reach. For example, on the baby changer, cot, crib or anywhere your baby could crawl.

Keep creams out of reach

Keep creams and similar items out of your baby's sight and reach. They could cause your child to be sick if eaten.

Constipation

Your baby's poo should be bulky and soft. Constipation is when babies have difficulty passing stools (firm poos). The stools may be firm dry pellets which do not soak into the nappy.

The poo passes more slowly. This may make your baby uncomfortable and disrupt their sleep.

Straining

Your baby may strain (grunt and become red in the face) when passing stools. This does not mean they are constipated if their poos are normal.

It is important to know what is normal for your baby. Some babies have several poos each day, while others poo only once a day or once every second day. What is important is that the poos are soft and that they are easy to pass.

Formula-fed babies tend to have bulkier poos and will need to poo more often than breastfed babies.

Breastfed babies

Breastfed babies rarely get constipated. Breastfed babies tend to have yellow-coloured seedy poos that are often quite soft. Newborn babies may poo after every breastfeed. Older breastfed babies may go up to a week without a bowel movement. This is not constipation once the stool is soft.

Causes of constipation

Your child could become constipated if they are:

- not drinking enough fluids (see below)
- not eating enough foods that contain fibre (see below)
- not active enough for their age
- ill or have a medical condition
- holding their poos in because it has hurt before

How to prevent constipation

Always follow instructions on the formula milk packaging.

Solids such as baby rice should never be added to a baby's bottle. These can choke your baby. They can also make your baby more likely to become constipated.

Fluids

Make sure your baby is having their daily fluid requirements (see below for babies under 6 months). Give them plenty to drink, such as breast milk or water. See pages 66 and 67 for information on suitable drinks.

Until your baby is aged 12 months, make sure to boil and cool the water first before giving it to them.

Foods that contain fibre

Give your child high fibre food as part of a well-balanced diet, such as:

- whole grain breakfast cereals, bread, pasta and rice
- fruit and vegetables
- beans

Dealing with constipation

If you think your baby or child is becoming constipated simple things may help.

Babies under 6 months

Make sure your baby is getting their daily fluid requirements. They should be taking in 700 ml of fluids each day, from breast milk or formula milk. You can massage your baby's tummy in a clockwise direction. Make firm but gentle circular motions from the belly button outwards.

You can try laying your baby on their back and gently moving their legs backwards and forwards in a 'bicycle' motion. Giving your baby a bath may help to relax their bowel.

> **Babies and children over 6 months**
>
> Offer your child plenty of fluids to drink at mealtimes and between meals. Offer them fruits like pears, kiwis, apples and strawberries. Make sure the consistency is right for your child's age. See page 61.

If you think your child is constipated, bring them to your GP.

> Contact your GP urgently if your child is constipated and has any of the following symptoms:
>
> * severe pain and distress on pooing (passing a stool)
> * bleeding from the back passage (rectum)
> * fever
> * vomiting
> * bloated tummy
> * losing weight or not gaining weight

Nappy rash

Nappy rash is a red, moist or broken area on your baby's nappy area. Most babies get nappy rash at some time in the first 18 months.

> **Your baby can get nappy rash if:**
> * they are left too long in a dirty or wet nappy
> * a rough nappy rubs against their skin
> * they have a thrush infection
> * their skin is sensitive to a soap, bath product or detergent like washing powder
> * baby wipes that contain alcohol are used
> * your baby is teething
> * your baby or toddler has recently been on antibiotics

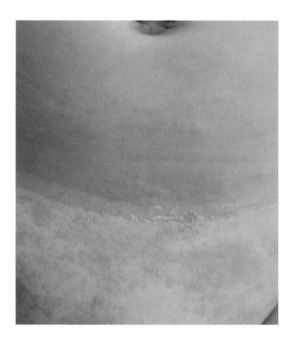

Dealing with nappy rash

Each time you change your child's nappy, gently clean their bottom with water and a soft cloth and pat it dry.

Leave their nappy off for half an hour and allow the skin of their bottom to air dry.

Add a thin layer of a protective barrier cream – your pharmacist or public health nurse will be able to recommend one.

Don't use bubble baths, talcum powder or any scented products on your baby. Sometimes it can be helpful to give the evening fluids early so that the nappy is not as wet overnight.

Bring your baby or toddler to your GP if they are in discomfort. Your GP can prescribe an ointment to help to heal the nappy rash.

Never apply raw egg or any other food directly onto your child's skin.

Dressing your child

0 to 1 year

Getting dressed is an opportunity for your baby to learn from your touch and voice. You can enjoy this time of smiling and talking to your baby.

Your child will start to move around more from 6 months on. They will need several sets of clothes. This is because they will spend more time on the go. They can get dirty very quickly from crawling and walking about.

1 to 2 years

Make dressing your toddler a game. Name their body parts and the clothes that cover them, like "your hat is for your head" or "your sock is for your foot". Your toddler learns different words and recognises the link between their clothes and where they fit.

When your toddler is walking steadily, bring them to a shoe shop to have their feet measured correctly. Every 3 to 4 months, go back to get their feet re-measured.

Child safety and clothes

Your child is at risk from anything placed on or caught around their neck. Risks include being choked, strangled or suffocated.

Never place any of the following on your baby or toddler:

- hair bands
- jewellery (including amber teething jewellery)
- strings
- cords
- belts
- ribbons
- soother clips
- ties
- clothes and hats with strings or cords attached

Remove bibs after feeding and before putting them down for a sleep.

Caring for teeth

Start taking care of your baby's mouth from birth. Clean their gums twice a day with a clean soft wash cloth or gauze.

Tooth brushing

Tooth brushing should be part of your child's daily routine. Good habits started early will last a lifetime.

When the first tooth appears:

- Use a small soft toothbrush and water only.
- Do not use toothpaste if your child is under the age of 2 – unless you have been advised to do so by a dentist.
- Brush your child's teeth twice a day – the brush before bedtime is the most important routine to establish, as food left on the teeth overnight can lead to decay.

If your child doesn't want their teeth brushed

Your child might resist having their teeth brushed, or want to do it themselves.

You can:

- sing a song as you brush their teeth, or
- reward them for letting you brush their teeth by allowing them to brush once you've finished.

You can find more tips and advice about pregnancy, babies and young children at **mychild.ie**

Protecting your child's teeth

Fluids

Only give your child fluids such as milk and water. Give cooled boiled water until your child is 1 year old.

Fruit juice and fizzy drinks

Juices for babies contain sugar, which can damage teeth. Never put sugary drinks, including fruit juice, into a bottle.

Never give fizzy drinks to your child. They contain a lot of sugar and acid.

Bottles

Start using a cup or free flow beaker from 6 months old and wean your child off bottle-feeding by 12 months.

Only give your child a bottle or feeding cup at feed times. Do not allow your child to move around with a bottle or feeding cup in their mouth.

Do not allow your child to sleep or nap with a bottle or feeding cup in their mouth.

Soothers

Avoid giving a soother (dodie, dummy or pacifier) after 12 months. If you give your child a soother, make sure it is clean. Do not dip it in sugar, syrup, honey or anything sweet.

Tips to help your child give up their soother

- Only use soothers at set times such as bedtime and remove the soother when your child is asleep.
- Take your child's soother out when they are trying to talk or busy playing.
- Give rewards but don't use food. For older children, try using a star chart to praise them.
- Don't replace lost soothers.
- Once your child has given up the soother, don't be tempted to give it back and stick with your decision – they will forget about it in time.

Tooth decay

Tooth decay is also called dental decay or dental caries. It is the destruction of the hard surfaces of the teeth. It happens when sugary foods and sugary drinks are broken down by bacteria in the mouth. This forms acids which destroy the tooth surfaces.

Teeth are at risk of decay from the time they appear in the mouth. Children with tooth decay are at risk of pain, infection and the early loss of their baby teeth. Food and drinks that contain sugar can cause tooth decay.

Did you know?

Tooth decay is the most common ongoing disease of childhood. It can be difficult to treat in very young children.

Preventing tooth decay

Avoid any foods and drinks that contain sugar as these can cause decay. Delay the introduction of sugary foods and drinks for as long as possible. This will help to prevent tooth decay. Bring your child for a visit to their dentist on a regular basis – normal dental check-ups can help prevent dental problems or spot them early on.

Where there is a choice, have your home connected to a public water supply that has fluoride – children and adults who live in areas where fluoride is in their water supply have better teeth than those who don't.

Healthy food for healthy teeth

- Encourage your child to eat foods that have a lot of calcium such as milk and cheese – calcium helps build strong teeth.
- Avoid sugary treats and read food labels carefully as sugar may also be called sucrose, glucose, fructose or maltose on labels. Remember: 'low sugar' or 'no added sugar' does not mean sugar-free.
- Encourage your child to eat fresh fruit as a healthy snack option.

Baby teeth

Healthy teeth allow your child to chew their food comfortably. They are also important for speech and for your child's appearance and self-confidence.

Baby teeth hold the space for the new permanent teeth to come into the mouth when your child is older. Your child may be 12 years old or more before their last baby tooth falls out, so these teeth need to be kept healthy for a long time.

Injuries to baby teeth

Falls, bangs and bumps are part of daily life for your toddler, and injuries to the baby teeth can easily happen. A fall on the mouth can loosen, break, knock out or push a baby tooth up into the gum.

This can cause damage to the developing adult (permanent) teeth. If your toddler injures or knocks out a tooth in a fall or accident, take them to their dentist to have their mouth and teeth checked. Do not try to put a knocked out tooth back in place as this could damage the adult tooth developing in the gum.

Toilet training

Toilet training is teaching your child to use the toilet instead of nappies. Many children are ready for this around the age of 2 although every child is different.

By around age 2, your child may be able to let you know that they need to go to the toilet or they have a dirty nappy. Wait until your child is ready before you begin toilet training.

Don't start at a time when other big changes are happening at home or in the family, for example if a new baby brother or sister has arrived.

Tips to help prepare

As you will have noticed by now, you have very little privacy with a small child and they even come in with you when you go to the toilet!

Watching you helps to prepare them for when they start to toilet train.

It is a good idea to:

- Leave a clean potty in the bathroom so your child gets used to seeing it.
- Start dressing your child in clothes that will be easy to pull up and down during potty training.

It can be frustrating when accidents happen, but they are part of the process.

Praise your child when they try, even if they do not go. Encourage them, and increase the praise when your child successfully uses the potty or toilet.

Vaccines

Vaccines or immunisations are a safe and effective way to protect your child against certain diseases. These diseases can cause serious illness or even death.

When your child is given a vaccine, their body responds by making antibodies to fight the disease.

Your child's vaccines are free of charge from your GP through the HSE. They are quick, safe and effective.

No parent likes the idea of their baby being given an injection. Be ready with a hug for your baby and the vaccination will be forgotten in seconds.

Your baby needs 5 visits to your GP to be fully vaccinated and protected against serious diseases by 13 months.

Three of these visits take place in their first 6 months. It is important that your baby gets their vaccines at the right age.

This means they are protected at the time when they are most at risk of becoming seriously unwell from the diseases.

Diseases your baby will be protected against

Primary **Chil**dhood Immunisation Schedule

Children born on or after 1 October 2016

Age	Vaccination
2 months	**Visit 1** — **6 in 1+PCV+MenB+Rotavirus** / 3 Injections+Oral Drops
4 months	**Visit 2** — 6 in 1+MenB+Rotavirus / 2 Injections+Oral Drops
6 months	**Visit 3** — **6 in 1+PCV+MenC** / 3 Injections

No Rotavirus vaccine on or after 8 months 0 days

Age	Vaccination
12 months	**Visit 4** — **MMR+MenB** / 2 Injections
13 months	**Visit 5** — Hib/MenC+PCV / 2 Injections

Remember to give your baby 3 doses of liquid infant paracetamol after the 2 and 4 month MenB vaccines.

1. Give 2.5 mls (60 mg) of liquid infant paracetamol at the time of the immunisation or shortly after.
2. Give a second dose of 2.5 mls (60 mg) 4 to 6 hours after the first dose.
3. Give a third dose of 2.5 mls (60 mg) 4 to 6 hours after the second dose.

 **Remember five visits to your GP (doctor)**

www.immunisation.ie
Order code: HNI00984

Feidhmeannacht na Seirbhíse Sláinte
Health Service Executive

Common side effects after vaccinations

Children may get:

- redness, soreness or swelling in the area where the injection was given
- irritable

If your child is very unwell after getting a vaccine, they may be sick for some other reason.

Contact your GP, GP practice nurse or public health nurse if you are worried about your child.

After the Meningitis B (MenB) vaccine

Your baby may develop a fever after MenB vaccine at 2 months and 4 months.

Give them 3 doses of liquid infant paracetamol as follows:

1. Give 2.5 mls (60mg) of liquid infant paracetamol at the time of the vaccination or shortly after.
2. Give a second dose of 2.5 mls (60mg) 4 to 6 hours after the first dose.
3. Give a third dose of 2.5 mls (60mg) 4 to 6 hours after the second dose.
4. If your baby still has a fever, give a fourth dose of 2.5 mls (60mg) 4 to 6 hours after the third dose.
5. Contact your GP if your baby still has a temperature after the fourth dose or if you are worried about them.

You don't need to give your child paracetamol when they get the MenB vaccine at 12 months as the risk of fever is less.

> Your public health nurse will give you information about vaccines and your child's immunisation passpost on their first visit to your home. Your GP and GP practice nurse will also give you information at the 2 week and 6 week check (see page 6).
>
> See immunisation.ie for more information about your child's vaccines.

When your child is sick

Most children get ill at some stage. At first, you may be nervous when your new baby is ill, but you will quickly become confident as you get to know their routine and learn how to help when they are sick.

Usually, you can care for your baby at home, as most illnesses pass quickly. Some common childhood illnesses are listed below with advice on what you can do to care for your child.

Contact your GP if you are unsure what to do or worried about your child.

Breastfeeding protects

Breastfeeding your child will help to protect them against fevers, coughs and colds and tummy upsets. If your child does get sick, it is important to continue to breastfeed them. Breastfeeding provides antibodies to protect your child against future illness. If you are formula feeding, continue to feed your child when they are sick.

Giving your child their usual milk feeds when they are ill is very important. Feeding will comfort your child and helps to ensure they get enough fluids.

When to get urgent medical help

When should I contact my GP or hospital emergency department?

You should contact your GP or nearest hospital emergency department if your child:

- has a purple or red rash that looks unusual
- has a raised or sunken soft spot (fontanelle) on their head
- has a temperature of 38°C or over
- appears much paler and sleepier then usual and is hard to wake up
- has an unusual, non-stop or high pitched cry or scream
- has a fit (convulsion)
- has difficulty breathing or is blue around the lips or face
- is not feeding normally or refuses to feed
- has unusually dry nappies or less than three wet nappies in one day
- has diarrhoea at each nappy change for more than 24 hours, or has bloody diarrhoea

> **Poison**
>
> If you think that your child has been exposed to or taken poison, stay calm but act quickly. Call the Public Poisons Information Helpline on 01-809 2166.
>
> The helpline is open from 8am to 10pm every day. Outside of these hours, contact your GP or hospital. In an emergency call 999 or 112.
>
> See poisons.ie

When should I call an ambulance?

Always call 112 or 999 if your child is seriously ill or injured, or their life is at risk.

Examples of medical emergencies include:

- difficulty breathing or is unconscious
- severe loss of blood, severe burns or scalds
- choking, fitting or convulsion
- severe head injury
- severe allergic reactions

Know your Eircode

It is a good idea to make a list of easy-to-follow directions to your home and put them in a visible place. An ambulance can find your home quickly if they have the Eircode. Find yours at eircode.ie

In an emergency it can be difficult to think clearly. Take the thinking out of it by preparing your directions and having your Eircode somewhere prominent in your home in case you need it.

Checking your child's temperature

You should check your child's temperature if they:

- have flushed cheeks
- feel hotter than usual when you touch them, especially their chest, forehead, back or stomach
- feel clammy or sweaty
- are crankier than usual

Using a digital thermometer

Digital thermometers are the most accurate way to measure your child's temperature. You can buy these in your local pharmacy, supermarket or online.

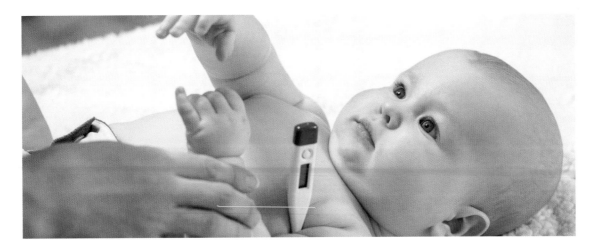

If your child is just out of a warm bath, or if they have been wrapped in warm clothing, wait for them to cool down before taking their temperature.

Most digital thermometers are designed to be used in your child's armpit.

1. Lie your baby flat or sit an older child comfortably on your knee, and put the thermometer in their armpit.
2. Gently hold their arm against their side to keep the thermometer in place. The instructions that come with the thermometer will let you know how long you need to hold it for but many digital thermometers beep when they are ready.
3. The display on the thermometer will tell you your child's temperature.
4. Other thermometers like ear (tympanic) thermometers or strip thermometers may not be as accurate but are very popular.

> **Mercury thermometers**
>
> Never use an old-fashioned glass thermometer containing mercury. These can break, releasing small splinters of glass and highly poisonous mercury.
>
> They're no longer used in hospitals and you can't buy them in shops. If your child is exposed to mercury, call the Public Poisons Information Helpline immediately.

Giving medicine to young children

Do:

✔ Always use the spoon or dosage syringe that comes with the medicine.

✔ Follow the dosage instructions very carefully.

✔ Give liquid medicines slowly to avoid choking.

✔ Keep medicines in their original containers.

✔ Keep all medicines, vitamins and food supplements out of children's reach and sight, and make sure lids are tightly closed.

Don't:

✗ Never give a medicine to a child without talking to a pharmacist, GP or public health nurse first.

✗ Don't use household spoons to give medicine – they come in different sizes and will not give your child the correct amount.

✗ Don't refer to medicine or vitamin tablets as 'sweets' as children may be tempted to find them to take more.

✗ Don't give aspirin to children under 16 unless a GP prescribes it – there is a risk of serious illness.

Paracetamol

Make sure you use the right type of paracetamol for your child's age. Check the correct dose for your child. It is dangerous to take too much paracetamol. Ask your pharmacist for advice and read all labels carefully.

Ibuprofen

You can give ibuprofen for pain and fever to children of 3 months and over who weigh more than 5kg (11lbs). Check the correct dose for your child's age.

Poison risk

Call the Public Poisons Information Helpline on (01) 809 2166 if you:

• are worried your child has taken too much medicine, or
• think that they may have taken medicine without your supervision

The helpline is open from 8am to 10pm every day.

Outside of these hours, contact your GP, GP out of hours service or hospital. In an emergency call 999 or 112.

Common illnesses

Fever

A fever is a high temperature of 38°C or above. Most high temperatures are caused by viral infections like colds and flus.

Occasionally a high temperature can be a sign that your child has more serious infection, like meningitis (see page 122).

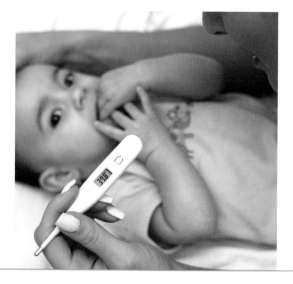

Reducing a fever

To help reduce your child's temperature, encourage them to drink lots of fluids such as their regular milk feeds. You may also need to give your child extra cooled boiled water to prevent dehydration. Remove their outer clothes to allow extra heat to escape from their body.

Medications

Medications such as liquid paracetamol or ibuprofen can be given to lower their temperature. But if your child is comfortable and appears well, medication may not be needed.

If you do give your child paracetamol or ibuprofen, always read the instructions. Ibuprofen is usually not advised for children under the age of 3 months. Keep all medicines out of sight and reach of children.

When to get help

Contact your GP immediately if your child is:

- under 3 months old and has a temperature of 38°C or over
- between 3 and 6 months old and has a temperature of 39°C
- showing other signs of being unwell such as drowsiness, refusal to feed or persistent vomiting

Febrile convulsion

A febrile convulsion is a seizure. It's sometimes called a fit. It can happen if your child has a very high temperature. The febrile convulsion may last for several minutes. Afterwards your child may be sleepy and limp.

During a febrile convulsion, your child may:

- become stiff and their arms and legs may begin to jerk
- lose consciousness and may wet or soil themselves
- foam at the mouth or vomit
- turn blue
- roll back their eyes

How to help your child

- Make a note of the time that the convulsion started.
- Lie your child on one side with their head tilted back slightly – this makes sure that their airway stays clear.
- Do not put anything in your child's mouth.
- Do not try to restrain them or shake them.
- When the seizure stops, try to lower your child's temperature to help them feel comfortable – make sure the room is warm but remove outer layers of clothing.

Most convulsions will stop after a few minutes. If this is the case, no further treatment of the seizure is needed but you should bring your child to a hospital emergency department that treats children as soon as possible. Sometimes they will need to be treated for whatever has caused their high temperature.

When to get help

Contact an ambulance by ringing 999 or 112 if:

- a seizure lasts for more than 5 minutes
- another seizure begins soon after the first one ends

Seeing your child have a febrile convulsion can be very frightening but they are usually harmless and most children make a full recovery.

Although there is unlikely to be anything serious wrong, it is still important to bring your child to a hospital emergency department that treats children for a check-up afterwards.

Croup

Croup is a type of cough that is common in young children up to the age of 3. It is caused by a viral infection of the voice box (larynx) and wind pipe (trachea). Your child may have a barking cough, be hoarse or make a harsh sound when breathing.

How to help your child

Croup usually gets better on its own after 48 hours. Until then, stay calm. If your child senses that you are stressed they may panic, which may make it harder for them to breathe.

- Reassure them and comfort them.
- Keep them upright and don't let them lie down.
- Give them fluids to drink such as water or their usual milk feeds.
- Don't give them any cough medicine, any herbal remedies or any medications that haven't been prescribed.
- Don't put your child in a steamy room or get them to inhale steam.

When to get help

The symptoms of croup are often mild, but they can become severe and things can change quickly. Occasionally children need to be admitted to hospital for treatment of their croup.

Always bring your child to the GP if you think they have croup. If their symptoms are severe or if they are finding it hard to breathe, bring them to your local emergency department that treats children.

Coughs and colds

Most coughs are caused by viruses like colds and flus. There is no quick way of getting rid of a cough, and they often last for up to 3 weeks.

If your child is drinking fluids and is in fairly good form, they can usually be cared for at home. Give them plenty of fluids to drink, such as their usual milk feeds, and offer food as usual.

Blocked nose

If your child's nose is blocked, you can wipe it gently. Saline drops can also be helpful, ask your pharmacist for advice.

If your child has a fever or if they are in discomfort, children's paracetamol or ibuprofen can help. Always read the instructions before giving these medications. Ibuprofen is not recommended for children under 3 months.

A warm and moist atmosphere can also help. Try taking your child into the bathroom which is still steamy from a hot bath or shower. Make sure to keep your child away from the hot water so they are not at risk of being scalded. You could also use a humidifier, which makes the atmosphere moist. If you do this, position the humidifier safely and out of reach of your children.

When to get help

Contact your GP if your child:

- has a cough or other cold symptoms lasting for more than 3 weeks
- is getting worse rather than better
- is rubbing or pulling at their ears and seems irritable
- seems wheezy (making noise when they are breathing)
- is refusing their milk feeds or not drinking fluids
- shows any other worrying symptoms like a rash or a headache

Go immediately to your GP or nearest hospital emergency department that treats children if your child is finding it hard to breathe.

Ear infections

An ear infection is an illness in the outer, middle or inner ear. It is usually caused by a virus. Most ear infections will clear up after 3 to 4 days. They can be painful so you may need to give your child liquid paracetamol or ibuprofen. Ask your pharmacist for advice.

Signs that your child has an ear infection may include:

- a temperature
- irritability and restlessness
- touching or pulling at the ear
- no interest in feeding

Older children may complain of earache and reduced hearing.

To help your child

- Do not use a cotton bud or anything else to poke inside their ear, as it may cause damage and pain.
- Do give children's paracetamol or ibuprofen to reduce the pain – but always read the instructions first.

When to get help

Take your child to the GP if:

- you are worried
- there is a discharge from the ear
- they seem very unwell or drowsy, or
- are not taking fluids

Antibiotics do not work against viral infections. They will not reduce the pain of an ear infection. Your GP will only prescribe an antibiotic if your child's ear infection has been caused by bacteria.

Vomiting

Small vomits (possets) after a feed can be normal and common in young babies. Your baby will grow out of this.

If your child is alert, behaving normally and feeding well, keep feeding them as normal and offer regular drinks of their usual milk or cooled boiled water.

When to get help

Contact your GP if:

- your child is repeatedly vomiting or unable to hold down fluids
- they have been vomiting for more than 2 days
- the vomiting is forceful or projectile
- the vomit is green or contains blood
- your child is under 3 months old and has a temperature of 38°C or higher
- your child is 3 to 6 months old and has a temperature of 39°C or higher, or
- your child has any signs of being dehydrated (dried out) such as drowsiness, not wetting many nappies or crying without tears

Babies or toddlers with vomiting should not go to crèche or a child minder until 48 hours after the last vomit.

Sticky eyes

It is very common for newborns and small babies to have 'sticky eyes'. Sticky eyes means that there is a yellow discharge from your child's eye. The white of the eye is not usually red, and your child is not usually distressed by this. Sometimes your child's eye can be crusted over and it can be hard for your child to open their eye.

How to help your child

Often no treatment is needed. Sometimes you may need to wipe or clean your child's eye. Always wash your hands before and after doing this. Use a sterile cotton ball dampened in saline solution to gently wipe your child's eye.

Wipe from the inside corner to the outside corner. Use a new cotton ball for each time you wipe.

Once you have bathed the eye, dry it using a different cotton wool ball and going from the inside corner to the outside.

When to get help

Contact your GP if:

- your baby's sticky eye is getting worse
- the white of your baby's eye is red
- your baby seems distressed and is doing things like rubbing their eyes a lot or seems to be in pain
- your baby does not like to open their eyes
- you are worried your baby might have conjunctivitis (the white of their eye is red) or if they have been in contact with someone who has conjunctivitis, such as an older sibling

If your child has sticky eyes but doesn't have these symptoms, mention it to your GP or public health nurse the next time you see them. They may show you ways to massage your baby's tear duct.

If your child's eye is still sticky after 12 months, visit your GP. They may refer your baby to see an ophthalmologist (a specialist eye doctor).

Thrush (candida)

Oral thrush or candida is an overgrowth of yeast fungus in your baby's mouth. It usually causes a white coating on your baby's tongue. It can also cause white patches in other parts of the mouth.

This coating usually does not brush away when you touch it. Oral thrush might affect your baby's feeding.

It can also be on your baby's bottom. It looks like a red rash with white spots or it can make the skin look like it is peeling.

When to get help

Contact your public health nurse, GP or pharmacist to find out how to treat thrush.

If you are breastfeeding and your baby has oral thrush, you could develop thrush on your nipples. You will normally be advised to continue breastfeeding but to apply an antifungal cream to your nipples.

It is very important to sterilise all bottles and soothers up to the age of 12 months. If an older child (over 12 months) gets thrush in their mouth, you should sterilise all bottles and soothers.

Tummy upsets or gastroenteritis

If your child has a tummy upset with vomiting, diarrhoea or both, then they can get dehydrated (dried out). It is particularly important to make sure they get enough fluid to drink.

How to help your child

Fluids

Continue offering your child their normal milk feeds, either breastfeeding or formula. Give them enough to drink in small sips of fluid. See pages 66 and 67 for more information on suitable drinks for your child.

Don't worry too much about food – fluids are the most important thing while your child is ill. If your child hasn't lost their appetite, it's fine for them to eat solid foods as normal.

Signs of dehydration

Look out for signs of dehydration such as not wetting many nappies, having a dry mouth, being drowsy or having no tears. If your child is starting to show mild signs of dehydration, ask your GP or pharmacist if you should give them oral rehydration solution.

Oral rehydration solution is a special powder that you make into a drink. It contains sugar and salts to help replace the water and salts lost through vomiting and diarrhoea.

High temperature or tummy pains

If your child is uncomfortable with a high temperature or tummy pains, you can give them liquid paracetamol.

Always read the label to make sure you give the correct dose to your child. Keep all medicines out of your child's sight and reach.

When to get help

Contact your GP if your child:

- is not drinking fluids or has any signs of dehydration
- has blood in their poo, or
- has had 6 or more episodes of diarrhoea in the past 24 hours, or 3 or more episodes of vomiting

The 48 hour rule

Children with vomiting or diarrhoea should not attend their crèche or childminder for 48 hours after their last vomit or runny poo.

Regularly wash your hands to avoid spreading any illness.

VTEC (Verotoxigenic E. coli)

VTEC (Verotoxigenic E. coli) is a serious type of gastroenteritis that can result in complications such as kidney failure.

A child infected with VTEC often has:

- diarrhoea (this might be bloody)
- stomach pains
- high temperature

About 1 in 10 children with VTEC can develop serious complications from it, where the kidneys stop working properly. This is called haemolytic uraemic syndrome (HUS).

> Bring your child to your GP if they have:
>
> - diarrhoea that is not setting, or
> - bloody diarrhoea

VTEC is very infectious, and can spread very easily in families, crèches and at childminders. This is why children with VTEC are not allowed to attend crèches or other childminding facilities until they are free of infection.

Go to the HSE's Health Protection Surveillance Centre website at hpsc.ie for more information on VTEC.

Chickenpox

Chickenpox is caused by the varicella-zoster virus. Your child can catch it by coming into contact with someone who has chickenpox.

If your child has not had chickenpox before, they can also catch chickenpox from someone with shingles.

The most obvious chickenpox symptom is a red rash that can cover the entire body.

Your child may have a fever and some mild flu-like symptoms before the rash appears. Flu-like symptoms can include feeling unwell, a runny nose and aches and pains.

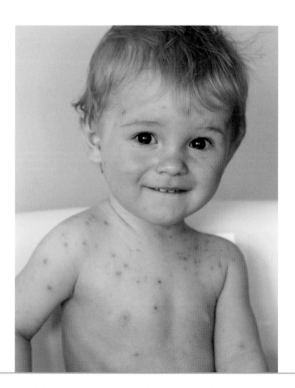

Chickenpox spots

Soon after the flu-like symptoms, an itchy rash appears. Some children may only have a few spots, but others are covered from head to toe.

Most healthy children recover from chickenpox with no lasting ill-effects. But some are unlucky and have a more severe illness than usual.

Unusual symptoms

Contact your GP straight away if your child develops any abnormal symptoms, for example, if:

- the skin surrounding the blisters becomes red and painful
- they start to get pain in the chest or have difficulty breathing
- your child is very unwell and you are concerned

Your child may need prescription medicine and possibly hospital treatment.

How chickenpox is spread

Chickenpox is highly contagious. This means it is very easy for your child to catch chickenpox if they never had it before. If someone in your home has chickenpox, there is about a 90% chance that others will catch it if they are not immune.

Chickenpox is spread by being in the same room as someone who has it. It can also be caught by touching clothes or bedding that has fluid from the blisters on it.

Chickenpox is most infectious from one to two days before the rash appears until the blisters have all crusted over. This means that a child could be spreading chickenpox before anyone knows that they have it.

It can take between 10 to 21 days after coming into contact with chickenpox for symptoms to appear.

How to help your child

The virus usually clears up by itself without any treatment.

There are ways of easing the itch and discomfort and steps you can take to stop chickenpox spreading.

Fever and pain

Give your child liquid paracetamol. It will help ease any pain they may be feeling and may help to control their temperature.

> Do not give your child ibuprofen if they have chickenpox. Research has found that serious skin reactions are more common in children with chickenpox who have been given ibuprofen.

Keeping hydrated

It is important to encourage your child to drink. Sugar-free ice-lollies are a good way of getting fluids into children. They also help to soothe a sore mouth that has chickenpox spots in it. See pages 66 and 67 for information on suitable drinks for your child.

Avoid any food that may make your child's mouth sore, such as salty foods.

Stop the scratching

Chickenpox can be incredibly itchy, but it's important that children do not scratch the spots. Not scratching will help them to avoid having scars after they recover.

- Get a soothing cream or gel in the pharmacy – this may help the itch and cool your child's skin.
- Ask your pharmacist if medication for the itch known as antihistamines might help – a sedating antihistamine can be used on children over the age of 1 and may help them to sleep at night.
- Dress your child in comfy clothes that won't make them overheat – getting too hot might make their itch worse.
- Bathe them in lukewarm water - a hot bath can make the itch worse.
- Pat their skin dry after a bath, don't rub.
- Keep their fingernails clean and short – you can also put socks over your child's hands at night to stop them scratching the rash as they sleep.

Your child will need to stay away from childcare and baby or toddler groups until all the spots have crusted over. This is usually 5 days after the spots first appeared.

It is a good idea to let your crèche or childminder know that your child has chickenpox, so they can alert other parents.

Complications

Some children are at risk of complications from chickenpox. These include:

- babies under the age of 1 month
- children with serious health problems such as heart and lung disease
- children on medications such as chemotherapy

Contact your GP if your child has any of these issues and you think they have been exposed to chickenpox.

When to get help

Call your GP urgently if your child has chickenpox and they have:

- redness, pain and heat in the skin around a blister or spot
- breathing problems
- symptoms of dehydration
- certain skin conditions like eczema
- headaches that don't go away after giving paracetamol, or are getting worse

Call your nearest hospital emergency department that treats children if your child has chickenpox and they:

- have trouble walking or are very weak
- are drowsy or hard to wake

Call 999 or 112 if your child has chickenpox and they have a fit or seizure.

Ring ahead if you are bringing your child with chickenpox to the GP or hospital. Your GP may arrange to see your child at a time when the surgery is quiet. This will reduce the risk of chickenpox spreading to vulnerable patients, for example, newborn babies.

Call your GP if you are pregnant and you know you are not immune to chickenpox or if you are not sure.

Hand, foot and mouth disease

Hand, foot and mouth disease is caused by a group of viruses which usually affects young children.

It causes blisters on hands, feet and in the mouth.

Children may also have a sore throat and high temperature. These symptoms last for seven to 10 days.

The vast majority of children who get hand, foot and mouth disease make a full recovery.

Did you know?

Not the same as foot and mouth disease

Hand, foot and mouth disease is not the same as foot and mouth disease, which affects cattle, sheep and pigs.

The two infections are unrelated. You cannot catch hand, foot and mouth disease from animals.

How it spreads

The virus is spread by coughs and sneezes, and is also found in the poo of infected children. Some children infected with the virus do not have symptoms but can still pass it to others.

How long before symptoms appear

Symptoms start 3 to 5 days after exposure to the virus.

How long children remain infectious

Children who are ill are infectious. They may also carry the virus in their poo for many weeks after they have recovered and this means they can continue to pass on infection.

How to prevent the spread of disease

The virus is found in poo. Make sure you wash your hands very carefully, especially:

- before preparing food
- after changing your child's nappy, or
- helping your child use the potty or toilet

How to help your child

There is no specific treatment for hand, foot and mouth disease – it is usually a mild illness that goes away of its own accord.

If a child feels unwell, liquid paracetamol may help. Always read the label. Keep it out of sight and reach of your children.

Make sure your child drinks plenty of fluids.

When to get help

Contact your GP if you are concerned or if your child has any of the symptoms listed on page 105.

Skin conditions

Eczema

Eczema is a very common skin condition that affects one in five children. It is caused by inflammation in the skin. It causes the skin to become itchy, dry, red and cracked.

The most common type of eczema is 'atopic eczema'. This is also sometimes called 'atopic dermatitis'. Most children with atopic eczema develop it before the age of one.

Bring your child to your GP if you think they have eczema.

Cradle cap

Cradle cap looks like dry, flaky or yellowish-crusted skin on your baby's scalp. Cradle cap will usually go away on its own.

Tips to help reduce the build-up of scales on the scalp

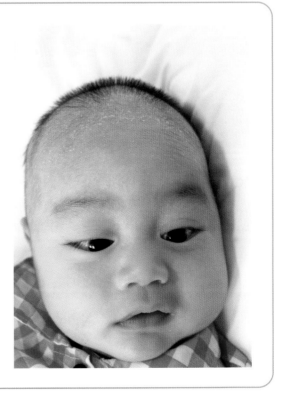

- Wash the scalp regularly with a baby shampoo, followed by gentle brushing with a soft brush to loosen scales.
- Soften the scales with baby oil first, followed by gentle brushing, and then wash off with baby shampoo.
- Soak the crusts overnight with white petroleum jelly, or vegetable or olive oil, and shampoo in the morning.

If these methods don't work, talk to your pharmacist about using a greasy emollient or soap substitute, such as emulsifying ointment.

Contact your GP if your baby's cradle cap:

- itches
- swells
- bleeds
- spreads to the face or body

Jaundice

Jaundice is when your baby's skin and eyes have a yellowish shade. Many babies get slightly jaundiced in the first few days after birth. This is because your baby's liver is not yet ready to fully break down blood cells.

Contact your midwife, GP or public health nurse if you think your baby is jaundiced.

Milk spots

Milk spots or milia are tiny white spots on your baby's face and neck. They are harmless tiny white cysts filled with a protein known as keratin. They will go away after a few weeks without any treatment.

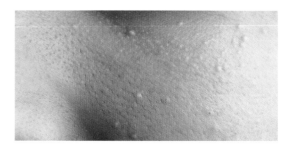

Other rashes

Babies can get rashes which are difficult to identify. These include heat rash – this fades once the baby is cooled down.

Bring them your child to your GP if they have a rash and you are unsure what is causing it.

Meningitis and septicaemia

Meningitis is an inflammation of the lining of the brain and spinal cord. There are two main types of meningitis: bacterial and viral. Septicaemia is a blood poisoning caused by bacteria.

Symptoms of meningitis or septicaemia

Children with meningitis or septicaemia won't usually have every symptom. They might not have a rash. Symptoms can appear in any order.

Think about meningitis or septicaemia if your child:

A high temperature or is cold

- has a temperature of 38°C or higher
- has cold hands and feet and is shivering

Dislikes bright lights
- squints or covers their eyes when exposed to light

Headache and neck stiffness
- has a very bad headache
- has a stiff neck

Pain or body stiffness
- has aches or pains
- has stomach, joint or muscle pain
- has a stiff body with jerking movements or a floppy lifeless body

Tummy symptoms
- is vomiting or refusing to feed

Confused, tired or irritable
- is very sleepy, lethargic, not responding to you or difficult to wake
- is irritable when you pick them up
- has a high-pitched or moaning cry
- is confused or delirious

Skin colour
- has pale or bluish skin

Unusual breathing
- is breathing fast or breathless

Soft spot
- has a tense or bulging soft spot on their head – the soft spot on their head is called the anterior fontanelle

Seizures
- has seizures

A rash
- a rash that doesn't fade when you press a glass tumbler against it (see next page)

Not every child has all these symptoms at the one time. Symptoms can occur in any order. Septicaemia can occur with or without meningitis.

How to check a rash

Check all of your child's body. Look for tiny red or brown pin-prick marks that do not fade when a glass is pressed to the skin.

These marks can later change into larger red or purple blotches and into blood blisters.

The rash can be harder to see on darker skin, so check on the palms of the hands or the soles of the feet.

Do the glass tumbler test

1. Press the bottom or side of a clear drinking glass firmly against the rash.
2. Check if the rash fades under the pressure of the glass.
3. If the rash does not fade, your child may have septicaemia caused by the meningitis germ.
4. Get medical help at once.

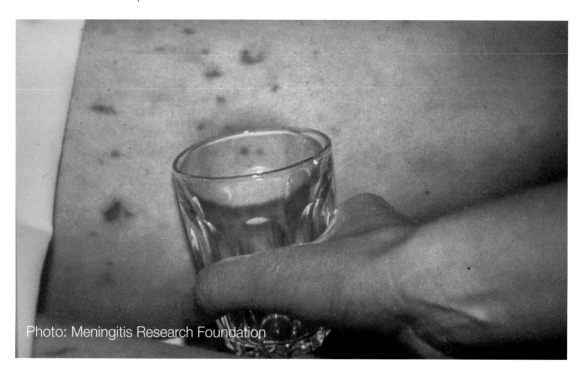

Photo: Meningitis Research Foundation

Getting medical help

If you think your child is seriously ill, call 999 or 112 or bring your child immediately to the nearest emergency department.

If you're not sure, contact your GP or GP out of hours service immediately and ask for an urgent appointment.

Bring your child immediately to your nearest hospital emergency department for children if:

- you are unable to contact your GP
- they are unable to see your child urgently

Trust your instincts. If you think your child is ill, get medical help at once.

> For more information on meningitis, go to the Meningitis Research Foundation website at meningitis.org or LoCall 1800 41 33 44.

Your child's growth and development

You will enjoy seeing how your baby grows and develops during their first weeks, months and years. Every child is unique, and grows and develops in their own time. There are milestones to measure along the way.

Your child's weight

It is normal for babies to lose some weight in the first two weeks after birth. Most babies are back at their birth weight by 2 weeks of age.

After this, steady weight gain is a sign that your baby is healthy and feeding well.

Your public health nurse and GP will help you if your baby has not regained their birth weight by 2 weeks or is losing weight. They may look for signs of medical problems.

If you are breastfeeding, your public health nurse will talk to you about how feeding is going and may ask to watch when you are giving a feed.

Checking your baby's weight

After the first 2 weeks, your child will be weighed by:

- your GP at the 6 week check
- your public health nurse at each developmental check

Many public health nurses also run 'well baby' clinics where you can bring your baby to be weighed.

Healthy weight gain

Most children are about three times their birth weight by one year of age – but this is just an average measurement. Your child may gain weight slower or faster than usual.

Sometimes weight gain can be slow if your child was premature or if they have been sick and off their feeds.

To help your toddler's healthy growth and development, they should have at least 3 hours of physical activity spread throughout the day. This can be anything that gets a toddler moving. Examples include crawling, walking, moving around the house, dancing, playing outside or exploring.

Your child's length and head circumference

Your child's length may be measured at:

- birth
- the 72 hour visit by the public health nurse
- the 6 week check with your GP or practice nurse
- each developmental assessment up to the age of 2 years

After the first month, your baby may increase in length by an average of 2½cm to 3cm (1 inch to 1½ inches) a month.

Your child's head circumference may be measured:

- around the time of birth
- at the 6 week check with your GP
- at the 3 month developmental assessment with your public health nurse

The head circumference gives an indication about how well your baby's brain is growing.

Growth charts

Your GP or public health nurse will record their measurements of your child's weight, length or head circumference. These results may be plotted on a growth chart.

Growth charts show the pattern of growth healthy children usually follow. There are different charts for boys and girls because they usually have slightly different growth patterns.

Centiles

When you look at a growth chart, you may notice that it has curved lines. These lines are called centiles. These show the average weight and height gain for children of different ages. The growth of your child will usually roughly follow a centile line.

Posture and movement

Every child is different and will develop at their own rate. This section is a guide to the milestones that your child will achieve as they develop.

The ages given are averages, and it is normal for children to gain one skill earlier than another. For example, some children are slow to walk but their speech may develop earlier than expected.

If your baby was premature, this can affect the way they develop. Your baby may need more appointments to check their development if they were premature.

Each child is different

What is important is how your child is developing overall. Try not to worry too much about the exact age at which certain milestones occur. For each milestone, there is a wide range of ages when children may reach it.

You can support your child's growth and development with many simple activities. If you are worried about your child's development or hearing, talk with your GP or public health nurse.

Your child's milestones

Here is a guide to your child's development, including their social and emotional development. Use it to see when your child may gain certain skills and learn new things.

1 to 2 months	3 to 4 months	5 to 6 months
Your baby may:	Your baby may:	Your baby may:
• hold their head up for short periods of time • bend their legs when they lie on their tummy • turn their head and eyes towards light	• kick vigorously • keep their head up with little or no support • lift up their head when you put them on their tummy with their arms on the floor • sit up straighter when you hold them in a sitting position • put weight on their feet when you hold them standing up • watch their own hands • be more awake and alert	• sit with support • roll from their front to their back • raise themselves on the palms of their hands when they lie on their tummy • grab small objects • look around constantly • put things in their mouth • play with their feet • hold up their arms so you can lift them

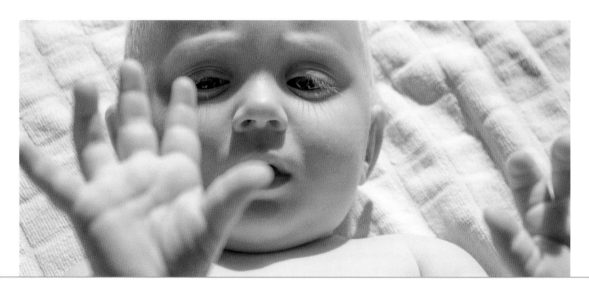

7 to 8 months	9 to 10 months	11 to 12 months
Your baby may:	Your baby may:	Your baby may:
<ul><li>sit up without being held or supported</li><li>twist around from side to side and lean forward while sitting</li><li>shuffle and wiggle about on the floor while sitting on their bottom</li><li>try to crawl on the floor</li><li>put their feet into their mouth</li><li>look to where a toy has fallen if it is close by</li></ul>	<ul><li>pull themselves up into a standing position by holding onto something solid such as an armchair</li><li>fall back down to the ground with a bump as they cannot lower themselves back down</li><li>attempt walking anytime from 8 to 20 months</li><li>use their index finger (next to their thumb) to jab and poke at small things like a dried raisin</li><li>stretch forward and grasp a toy with both hands while sitting down without falling over</li><li>show that they are annoyed about something by holding their body stiff or rigid when you pick them up</li></ul>	<ul><li>walk around the furniture while holding on to it</li><li>start walking without holding on to the furniture but with one hand holding yours</li><li>drop and pick up toys</li><li>help with being dressed by holding out their arm or leg</li><li>begin to stop drooling and putting objects into their mouth</li></ul>

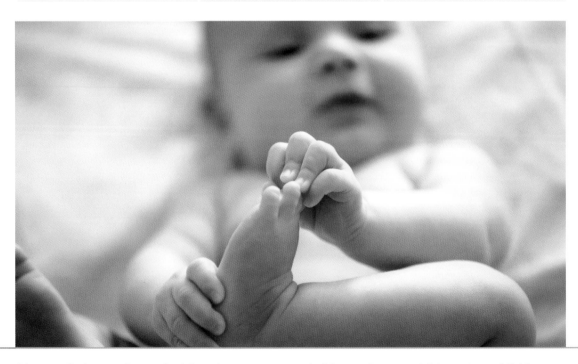

13 to 18 months (1 to 1½ years)	19 to 24 months (1½ to 2 years)
Your toddler may:	Your toddler may:
• walk about with their arms slightly out to balance themselves at first • carry things like a toy while they are walking • fall down when they learn to walk about • crawl upstairs and come down backwards • hold a crayon in their fist to scribble • throw toys and objects to the floor and watch where they fall • put things in and out of boxes or plastic jars	• fall down less often when walking or running about • push or pull toys along the floor • squat down to pick up fallen toys • enjoy climbing up on furniture, such as chairs or the table, as they explore and climb with no sense of danger • walk upstairs with help and creep downstairs backwards or sit on their bottom and bump down step by step • hold small objects like crayons more firmly in one hand when drawing and scribbling • follow you around the home and enjoy helping with everyday chores

Tummy time

Babies need to be physically active several times each day, especially through interactive floor-based play. This means playing on the floor with you and toys appropriate to their age. Floor-based play includes tummy time.

Tummy time should start from birth. Try to do tummy time three to four times a day for short periods of time.

Tummy time helps to strengthen their head, neck and back muscles. It also lets your baby experience feeling to the front of their body.

Place your baby on a firm and flat surface for tummy time. During the day you can place your baby on their tummy with their hands out at either side to support themselves. You must stay close to your baby while they are in this position.

If your baby falls asleep when on their tummy, always place them onto their back to reduce the risk of cot death.

Your baby shouldn't be inactive or in a restricted position for any longer than 1 hour, except when sleeping.

See page 167 for a guide on how to play with your baby and toddler and how this helps their development.

Here are some ways to put tummy time into your baby's routine:

Tummy-to-tummy

Lie down on the floor or a bed. You can lie flat or prop yourself up on pillows. Place your baby on your chest or tummy so that you're face-to-face. Always hold your baby firmly for safety.

Eye-level smile

Get down level with your baby to encourage eye contact.

Roll up a blanket and place it under their chest and upper arms for added support.

Lap soothe

Place your baby face-down across your lap to burp or soothe them.

A hand on your baby's bottom will help them feel steady and calm.

Tummy-down carry

Carry your baby 'tummy down'. To do this, slide one hand under the tummy and between the legs. Nestle your baby close to your body.

Tummy minute

Place your baby on their tummy for one or two minutes every time you change them.

Information and images reproduced from pathways.org.

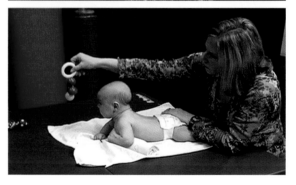

How your child communicates with you

From birth to 12 months

0 to 3 months

Your newborn baby has a wide range of ways to communicate with you.

How they comunicate

Crying is one way your baby communicates with you that they need something. Your baby also communicates through facial expressions and body movements. Through these behaviours, your baby is communicating important messages about their feelings to you.

> ### Most interested in you
>
> Your baby is learning to pay attention to new sights, sensations and sounds. Above anything else, your baby is most interested in looking at your face and hearing your voice. You are your baby's best toy!
>
> You are the most important person in your baby's life. Your baby can express their interest in you by looking at you and beginning to smile.

Cooing

Your baby is learning how to take turns in conversations. They can make sounds like "eee" and "ahhh". This is called cooing.

4 to 6 months

Your baby can now make even more noises to get your attention. They can use different noises to communicate their feelings.

Babbling

You may notice your baby beginning to babble, for example "ba ba ba" or "da da da". This is your baby's way of using their sounds. They are letting you know they are interested in having a conversation with you.

Reacting to voices

You may notice your baby gets excited when they hear voices, especially yours! They might express this excitement by kicking their legs, waving their arms or making noises.

You might notice your baby starting to laugh and squeal with enjoyment.

Touch

Your baby can reach out and grasp objects that are close by. They often enjoy reaching out to touch your face, building their connection with you.

6 to 12 months

Your baby's communication skills are growing dramatically.

You might notice your baby puts lots of sounds together by using either:

- babbling, for example "ma ma ma" or "da da da", or
- longer babbling that includes longer sequences of sounds, for example "ada abu mada kala…"

You might also notice your baby:

- pointing at an object that interests them and then getting your attention by looking at you and back at the object
- looking at you when you talk or when they hear their name being called
- copying some sounds you make, such as coughing or making 'raspberries'
- enjoying games like 'peek a boo' or 'row the boat' on your lap
- starting to understand some words like "bye bye", "no" or "all gone", especially when you use a gesture at the same time
- understanding the names of familiar objects or people, like "mammy", "daddy", "teddy" or "cup".

Ways to support your baby's communication

Your baby loves following your cues. The relationship you have is the most important way to help their language and communication develop.

Watch and tune into your baby's facial expressions, eye gaze and body movements. Wonder about what your baby is thinking, feeling or showing interest in.

Respond to your baby by:

Talking

Talk to them about what they are doing, for example "You're looking at the light."

Going slowly

It's important to match your baby's pace when you are playing together. Your baby's brain needs time to process new experiences and words.

Getting face to face

Your baby will love looking at your eyes and smiling. This helps their speech and language to develop. Find a comfortable distance (approximately arm's length) that allows your baby to focus on your face.

Listening

Listen to your baby. Leave little pauses for your baby to take their turn. This shows them that you are interested in their thoughts and feelings.

Copying your baby and waiting

Copy their sounds or actions and wait. For example, if your baby says "bababa", repeat back "bababa" with enthusiasm. Wait to see if your baby is interested in taking another turn.

Speaking your native language

Talk to your baby in your native language. This is best for their speech and language development. This will also nurture your important relationship with your baby.

In two-parent families, this could mean your baby is exposed to two or more languages from birth. For example, if one parent speaks in their native Polish and the other parent talks to them in their native English.

Comforting your baby when they cry

Providing lots of love and comfort helps your baby feel safe and secure with you. Responding to your baby's cries helps build healthy self-esteem. It also sets a strong foundation for their growing communication development.

Other fun activities to try

Songs and nursery rhymes

Sing songs and nursery rhymes with your baby.

Picture books

Snuggle up and share a picture book together. Allow your baby to hold the book. Notice what your baby is interested in and talk about that for example, "You see the monkey!"

At this stage, this is more important than reading the words in the book.

Play on the floor

Your baby can learn so much language through playing with you. At this stage, your baby might enjoy touching or holding little toys with different feels, like soft blocks or a rattle.

Pace your play to suit your baby. You can repeat lots of new words, for example "shake shake" or "the ball feels squishy!"

Peek-a-boo

Social games like "Peek-a-boo" are a lot of fun and a great way to encourage your baby's communication and concentration.

Sensory books

Your baby will really enjoy 'touch and feel' sensory books. Allow your baby to hold the book and notice how they look at the pictures and touch the pages. Notice what your baby is interested in and talk about that, for example "the cat feels furry!"

Blocks

Your baby might enjoy banging blocks together or putting blocks into a cup. They might like to play with a ball, a pop-up toy or bubbles with you.

These games allow you to repeat lots of new words such as "the block is in the cup" or "pop the bubble".

From 12 to 24 months

This is an amazing time in your toddler's language development. During this period, one of the most exciting milestones arrives – their first words.

There is often a huge spurt of language growth between 12 to 24 months. During this time, your toddler's understanding of language is growing fast. They are beginning to:

- understand some simple words and short phrases such as "it's bath time" or "where's the ball?"
- understand some simple action words, for example "who's eating?" or "who's sleeping?"

- identify some body parts, for example eyes, nose, mouth, hands
- recognise and point to familiar objects, people or pictures when asked, for example "where's teddy?" or "where's daddy?"

> Your toddler will begin to use more and more words. You will notice your toddler:
>
> - using single words to express their thoughts, feelings or ideas – they might point and say "mama" to communicate "there's mammy"
> - combining babble and real words to try to form sentences
> - pointing at things that interest them and asking "what's that?" – it helps your child to build their growing vocabulary when you answer these questions
> - saying the same words over and over to practise their new vocabulary
>
> As they approach 2 years of age, your toddler may start joining two words together, for example "daddy ball" or "teddy jump".

How to support your toddler's communication

Just like when they were a baby, your toddler's communication will thrive through your spending time with them. It is important that you continue to tune into their facial expressions and sounds.

Show interest in what they are doing and respond to them by:

- describing your daily activities together, for example "that's the car" and "we're changing your nappy"
- adding words to your toddler's sentences, for example if they say "kick ball" you could say "yes, mammy is kicking the ball" – this helps them to use longer sentences when they are ready

Use actions with your words

For example, wave when you say "bye bye" or shake your head when you say "no". This makes it easier for your toddler to understand your words and gives them more ways to communicate with you too.

Give "it" a name

Instead of saying "there it is", you could say "there's the ball" or "there's the bubble". This will help them to become familiar with a range of specific words.

Speak slowly and clearly

When talking with your toddler, speak slowly and clearly, so that they have the best opportunity to hear the sounds at the beginning, middle and end of the words. This will help to develop their speech sounds.

Stay calm when they're being challenging

Staying calm will help your toddler to learn how to deal and emotions. It also encourages good self-esteem and sets a strong foundation for their growing communication and later speech and language development.

Use words to describe your toddler's feelings

Name the emotions your toddler is experiencing, for example, happy, excited, sad or upset. This gives your child the words to understand and talk about their own and others' feelings. This is very important for your child's emotional awareness and development.

Limit screen time

Screens can be smartphones, gaming devices, tablets, computers and televisions. Try to limit screen time to under one hour per day for 18 to 24 month olds. It is not recommended for children under 18 months to have any screen time.

Watching too much on screens can take time away from special interactions with your toddler that are important for speech and language development.

Limit soothers

Try to limit your toddler's use of soothers, especially when they are awake. Soothers can lead to difficulties with their teeth and speech.

Fun activities to try with your toddler

Ideas include:

Action songs and nursery rhymes

Sing action songs and nursery rhymes with your toddler. Repeat the same songs and go slowly, so that your toddler can become familiar with the rhythm.

"This little piggy went to the market…" is a fun rhyme to sing during nappy change or after bath time. When your toddler starts using their first words, try leaving out the last word of the rhyme for your toddler to say, for example: "They all fall…"

Books

Most toddlers enjoy books with simple stories or about their favourite characters. Encourage them to join in for repetitive lines of the story. It is best to follow your toddler's interest in the book – this may involve describing the pictures instead of reading the story.

Floor play

Play on the floor with your toddler, they can learn so much language through play.

Other games

Your toddler might enjoy imaginary games, jigsaws, painting and much more. These games allow you to interact and talk with them and to support their growing speech and language development.

All children are individuals and develop at different rates. The information in this book is a guide only.

If you are worried about your toddler's communication development, contact your:

- public health nurse
- GP

Possible signs your child is not developing as expected

All children develop at their own pace. Try not to compare your child with other children.

If you are worried about your child's development at any stage, always speak to your public health nurse or GP. Sometimes children learn a new skill like waving, and then seem to become bored of it. This can be normal.

But if your child seems to be losing skills that they had it is a good idea to speak with your public health nurse or GP. For example, if your child stops talking.

Trust your instincts. You know your child better than anyone else.

If your child was premature

Remember that if your baby was premature, they may follow a different pattern of development. Sometimes your paediatrician, public health nurse or GP will assess their milestones based on their due date, and not the date they were actually born.

By the age of 2 or 3, the development of premature babies tends to be similar to that of other children their age, and you can start using their actual age when looking at their milestones. Your paediatrician, paediatric nurse, public health nurse and GP will give you more information.

Things you should look out for

0 to 6 months

Talk to your GP or public health nurse if your child:

- does not move, or appears not to be using both arms and both legs
- does not hold their head up by 3 months
- does not seem to see or hear things
- has an unusual cry, for example, high-pitched
- is not smiling by 6 to 8 weeks
- keeps one or both hands clenched into a fist after 4 months

6 to 12 months

Talk to your GP or public health nurse if your child:

- is very reluctant to start solid foods from about 6 to 7 months on
- does not hold toys when offered to them
- is not able to sit unsupported by 10 months
- does not use both hands equally
- is not crawling or moving forward in some way
- does not smile or laugh out loud
- does not make different sounds when they speak
- does not turn towards you when you call their name
- does not make eye contact with you
- does not show pleasure when seeing you and other familiar people
- is constantly irritable and unable to soothe themselves or gain comfort from you
- has difficulty establishing a sleeping, waking and feeding pattern
- fails to gain weight even though they seem healthy

1 to 2 years

Talk to your GP or public health nurse if your child:

- is mainly silent when playing or does not babble a lot
- is not able to point to objects and toys that you name
- is not walking by 18 months or walks on their toes only
- does not imitate actions or words
- is not using some words or phrases by 18 months
- does not follow simple instructions by 2 years old
- does not listen when others are talking
- does not show any anxiety or upset when they are separated from you
- has difficulty interacting with you and other caregivers, including not making eye contact with you
- clings to you a lot and does not like changes in their routine
- does not show affection to familiar people
- is not responding to the limits you set and can be very stubborn or defiant in their contacts with you and others

Ask your public health nurse to perform an 'ages and stages questionnaire' on your child if you are concerned about any aspect of their development. This will look at your child's development in more detail.

Caring for your child with special needs

If your child has special needs or a long-term illness, this can bring extra adjustments to your family's life. As a parent you may have difficult feelings to cope with. You may also have to make additional decisions for your child and your family.

Your GP and public health nurse are there to help. They can offer information and support to guide you. They can also refer you to other services that you may need.

Useful websites

When your child is diagnosed with a particular condition, you may look for information online. You should always remember that while the internet is a great source of information, there is also a lot of information that is out of date, unreliable or incorrect.

The information you find online may not be relevant to your child's own needs, even if it is about the same condition. Each child is different.

If you have recently found out about your child's disability or developmental delay, you may find informingfamilies.ie helpful.

Talking to other parents

Although everyone's experience is different, it can be helpful to speak to other parents who have children with needs similar to your child's.

They are likely to have been through the same emotions and pathways. They may be able to offer you some practical advice.

The Special Needs Parents Association is run by parents to provide families of children with disability or special needs with support and information. See specialneedsparents.ie

Services for children with special needs

When a child is diagnosed with a disability or there are concerns that their development may be delayed, it is important that parents are supported to provide the extra care their child needs to reach his or her potential.

Your child may need services such as physiotherapy or speech and language therapy. Parents can find out about how to encourage their child's development and get advice on practical issues. What services you and your child are offered depends on the needs of your child.

Health services for children with a disability or developmental delay are provided by the HSE itself or by certain voluntary organisations which receive funding from the HSE.

Many children with delays in their development can have their needs met by their local HSE primary care services such as a community speech and language therapist or physiotherapist.

Children's disability teams provide services for children with more complex needs, who require the support of a team of professionals working closely together.

Children's disability services vary across the country. You can see a list of the services in your area at hse.ie/childdisability or talk to your public health nurse about what's available near you and how to get your child referred to a service that may help them.

Financial entitlements

Benefits and entitlements

Information on benefits and entitlements is available on citizensinformation.ie

Domiciliary care allowance

This is a monthly payment made to the carer of a child with a severe disability who lives at home. See welfare.ie

Carer's benefit

This is a payment made to people who leave the workforce to care for a person or people who need full-time care and attention. See welfare.ie

Carer's allowance

This is a payment to people on low incomes who are looking after a person who needs support because of age, disability or illness. See welfare.ie

Carer's support grant

This is an annual grant made to carers. It is paid automatically to people getting carer's allowance (full-rate or half-rate), carer's benefit or domiciliary care allowance. See welfare.ie

Financial entitlements continued

Long term illness scheme

This includes free drugs, medicines and medical and surgical appliances for the treatment of certain conditions. The scheme does not depend on your income or other circumstances. See hse.ie

Medical card for people receiving domiciliary care allowance

If you have a child for whom you are getting domiciliary care allowance, they are eligible for a medical card without a means test. See hse.ie

Incapacitated child tax credit

This is a tax credit if you have a child who is permanently incapacitated. See revenue.ie

Housing grants for adapting your home

A housing adaptation grant is available where changes need to be made to a home to make it suitable for a person with a physical, sensory or intellectual disability or a mental health difficulty. Contact your local city or county council for details.

'Better Energy Warmer Homes' scheme

Funds are available to make the homes of families receiving the domiciliary care allowance warmer and more energy efficient. See seai.ie

Tax reliefs for drivers and passengers with disabilities

There is a range of tax reliefs for the costs of buying and using a specially constructed or adapted vehicle for drivers and passengers with a disability. See revenue.ie

Equipment

Depending on their particular needs and difficulties, your child might benefit from equipment such as a walking aid or a special seat.

A health professional such as an occupational therapist can help you find out what would be the best option for your child and how to apply for it to be supplied or funded.

If you have a medical card or long term illness card, the HSE may provide equipment which has been prescribed by a health professional. If you have private health insurance, funding for some equipment may be covered so check with your insurer.

Pre-school supports

The Access and Inclusion Model (AIM) supports children with disabilities to access and fully participate in their local preschool.

If your child needs support to attend, including equipment or expert advice from an early years specialist, the preschool will make an application with your help and permission to AIM.

See aim.gov.ie for more information and talk to your pre-school provider.

Home supports

Caring for a child with special needs, especially if they have complex medical needs, can put a lot of extra pressure on parents and carers.

Home support is when a family support worker takes over care of your child for a period of time to allow you some time off. The availability of this service varies across the country, so talk to your public health nurse or your child's disability team to find out if it is available.

Assessing your child's needs

Your child is entitled to an assessment of need under the Disability Act if you think that they have a disability. You can contact an assessment officer through your local HSE health centre. See hse.ie for more information.

Please note that it is not essential to go through the assessment of need process to access services for your child – they can be referred directly.

See hse.ie/progressingdisabilityservices for more information.

Your child's eyesight

Your baby should have sight from birth. Soon after your baby is born a doctor or specialist midwife will shine a light into your baby's eyes. This is a screening examination to look for cataracts.

Cataracts

Cataracts (when the lens of the eye is clouded) are rare in newborns. Screening improves the chances of this being picked up early. This means your baby will be treated if needed.

Your child's age	Your child may
0 to 6 weeks	• start to focus their gaze – they love looking at faces
6 to 8 weeks	• look at you • follow your face and smile back when you smile • follow a brightly coloured toy that is held about 20cm away • move both eyes together
2 to 6 months	• enjoy looking at bright colours and following moving objects with their eyes
By about 6 months	• look around them with interest • see across a room • notice and reach out for small coloured blocks 2.5cm wide or other objects that are placed 30cm in front of them • recognise familiar toys and people that are about 2 to 3 metres away
By about 9 months	• reach out to touch objects and toys that they see in front of them • look at small things, such as crumbs of bread, that are 30cm in front of them • use their hands and eyes to co-ordinate poking at the crumbs • recognise familiar people who are across the street
By about 1 year onwards	• recognise and point to objects and toys that they want • notice people, traffic or animals that are moving about outside and will watch them with interest for a while

If you have concerns about your child's eyes

Some babies are born with eye problems or develop eye problems at an early age. Some of these problems can be treated if they are identified early. Your child's eyes will also be checked at their developmental assessments with the public health nurse (see page 8).

Contact your public health nurse or GP if you notice something wrong with the appearance of your child's eyes or think they cannot see properly.

Your child's hearing

Newborn babies will have their hearing screened in the hospital. If your baby was born at home, your midwife will arrange this. Shortly after birth, babies should startle to sudden loud noises, like a loud clap or a door slamming. Babies will respond by blinking or opening their eyes wide.

What your child can hear

Your child's age	Your child may
By 0 to 3 months	• be startled by loud sounds • notice sudden noises like the noise of the vacuum cleaner and should pause and listen when it is turned on • quieten or smile at the sound of your voice, even when they can't see you
4 to 6 months	• turn their head to follow sounds • move their eyes in the direction of sounds • respond to changes in the tone of your voice • notice toys that make sounds
6 to 8 months	• turn their head at once towards a parent or carer when they hear a familiar voice • turn towards and locate very quiet sounds made at either side of them if they are not too distracted by what is going on in front of them
About 9 months	• pay attention to what they're doing but be easily distracted by sounds • notice everyday sounds • make eye contact readily • try to maintain interaction with carer through eye contact and cooing or babbling • babble using a variety of sounds • respond to their own name • begin to respond to requests such as "come here" or "want more?" • use speech or non-crying sounds to get and keep attention
12 months to 2 years	• point to a few parts of their body when asked • follow simple commands and understand simple questions ("roll the ball," "kiss the baby" or "where is your shoe?") • listen to simple stories, songs or rhymes • point to pictures in a book when named

If you are concerned about your child's hearing

If you are worried about your child's hearing at any time, contact your public health nurse or GP to talk about your concerns.

Speech and language

You baby's speech and language development is linked to your baby's ability to hear.

What your child should be able to do between birth and 1 year

Hearing and understanding	Speech and language
Birth to 3 months	
<ul><li>Startles to loud sounds.</li><li>Goes quiet or smiles when spoken to.</li><li>Seems to recognise your voice and goes quiet if crying.</li></ul>	<ul><li>Makes pleasure sounds (cooing or gooing).</li><li>Cries differently for different needs.</li><li>Smiles when they see you.</li></ul>
4 to 6 months	
<ul><li>Moves eyes in direction of sounds.</li><li>Responds to changes in tone of your voice.</li><li>Notices toys that make sounds.</li><li>Pays attention to music.</li></ul>	<ul><li>Babbling sounds more speech-like with many different sounds, including p, b and m.</li><li>Chuckles and laughs.</li><li>Vocalises excitement and displeasure.</li><li>Makes gurgling sounds when left alone and when playing with you.</li></ul>

7 months to 1 year

Hearing and understanding	Talking
• Enjoys games like peek-a-boo and pat-a-cake. • Turns and looks in direction of sounds. • Listens when spoken to. • Recognises words for common items like "cup", "shoe", "book" or "juice". • Begins to respond to requests such as "come here" or "want more?"	• Babbling has both long and short groups of sounds such as "tata upup bibibibi". • Uses speech or non-crying sounds to get and keep attention. • Uses gestures to communicate (waving, holding arms to be picked up). • Imitates different speech sounds. • Has one or two words ("hi", "dog", "dada" or "mama") around first birthday, although sounds may not be clear.

What you child should be able to do between 1 and 2 years

• Points to a few body parts when asked. • Follows simple commands and understands simple questions like "roll the ball", "kiss the baby" or "where's your shoe?" • Listens to simple stories, songs and rhymes. • Points to pictures in a book when named.	• Says more words every month. • Uses some one-word or two-word questions like "where kitty?", "go bye-bye?" or "what's that?". • Puts two words together like "no cat" or "mommy book". • Uses many different consonant sounds at the beginning of words.

Reprinted with permission from How Does Your Child Hear and Talk © 2013. American Speech-Language-Hearing Association.

Your child's teeth

Teething and gums

Teeth don't usually appear until your baby is 6 months or later. They may show signs of teething from about 13 weeks.

Your child should have most of their 20 baby teeth by the time they are 2-and-a-half years old.

Every child is born with a complete set of 20 baby teeth growing under their gums.

Signs your baby is teething

Your baby may:

- have red and flushed cheeks
- dribble – wipe this away from the skin folds on their neck because this can cause soreness
- chew on their fists or on their toys more than usual
- have sore and tender gums and cry more
- have a nappy rash

Contact your public health nurse or GP if your child has a raised temperature, diarrhoea or generally seems unwell. This is not caused by teething.

Helping your teething baby

It's upsetting to see your baby in discomfort from teething. Comforting and playing with them will help distract them.

Here are some other ways you can help:

- try giving your baby something to chew on such as a cool teething ring
- massage your child's sore gums with a sugar-free teething gel
- use mild sugar-free pain relief if your child wakes at night and is irritable
- give cold water to drink – this helps to keep babies hydrated and may also soothe their gums (remember to boil and cool water before giving it to a baby under 12 months)
- give healthy foods to chew on – but only do this if they're 6 months or older and stay close to your baby when they are eating in case they choke

Teething rings

Chewing on a cool and clean teething ring can help soothe your baby's gums as well as distracting them from the pain.

You can cool some teething rings in the fridge. Always check the product instructions for how long to cool the ring. Never put the ring in the freezer as this could damage your baby's gums. Keep a spare clean teething ring in the fridge.

Let your baby hold the teething ring. Never place it on a string around their neck as this might strangle them.

You can also give your baby a cold wet facecloth to chew on.

Teething gels and pain relief

Sugar-free teething gels are available over the counter from the pharmacy. They contain a mild local anaesthetic which helps numb any pain. These are for babies older than 4 months.

Always make sure the product you use is suitable for your baby's age and ask your pharmacist for advice.

If your baby is still in discomfort after using teething gels, consider giving them sugar-free paracetamol or ibuprofen medication for babies. Don't use ibuprofen medication if your baby is under the age of 3 months.

Contact your GP or pharmacist for information on the safe use of gels and pain relief.

Homeopathic teething products

There are some unlicensed homeopathic products sold online. These are not safe to use for babies.

Research into these products shows that they may cause serious side effects. These include difficulty breathing, seizures, agitation, excessive sleepiness, constipation and difficulty urinating.

This warning does not apply to Nelson's homeopathic teething products sold in Ireland with the brand name of 'Teetha'.

Do not use teething jewellery

Never use amber teething jewellery such as necklaces, bracelets and anklets. These products are unsafe. They are a potential choking hazard to any child less than 3 years of age.

How teeth grow

Your child's first two teeth usually come through on the bottom gum.

Thumb-sucking

Sucking their thumb soothes some small children. Some young children develop this habit around 18 months old and will stop it by four years old. Thumb-sucking is only a problem if it continues beyond this age. This is because the sucking may affect the shape of the permanent front teeth.

It is also important that you regularly wash your child's hands. Regular hand washing can help stop infections transferring from their hands to their mouths.

Ask your dentist, GP, GP practice nurse or public health nurse for more advice about caring for your child's teeth.

Your baby's social and emotional world

The relationship between you and your child in the early years of their life provides the foundation for good health and well-being throughout the rest of their life.

How your baby develops as a person

You are building a bond with your baby from the moment they are born. The way you hold your baby closely, make eye contact, speak with them, touch and comfort them are all part of building this loving and trusting relationship.

Responsive parenting

Your child's social, emotional and behavioural development is influenced by the way you listen and respond to them and by the way they respond to you. From an early age, you are starting to learn and identify your baby's cues around tiredness, hunger and possible pains. It is important to tune into these cues as they will help you to get to know your baby.

Listening to cues

Cues will help you to soothe and comfort your baby and identify what they need. Every baby is special and unique and has their own personality. You will get to know from your baby's cues what touches, sounds and environments they enjoy.

Feeling safe helps them to be confident

As your child grows, it is important that you provide a safe, secure and nurturing environment for them to develop. They will at first be dependent on you, and become gradually more independent.

As a parent, it is important to know what to expect as your child grows so that you can support and help them to grow to be confident, happy and secure.

Milestones for your baby's social and emotional development

Baby's age	Your baby may
1 to 2 months	• respond to your voice • cry, smile and coo • look at faces • quieten when picked up (most of the time)
3 to 4 months	• give warm smiles and laughs • cry when upset and seek comfort • show excitement by waving arms and legs
5 to 6 months	• be friendly with strangers, but may show slight anxiety when you or another trusted adult is out of sight • know and respond to familiar faces
6 to 9 months	• begin to show fear of things that did not bother them before this, such as heights or going for a bath • get very attached to you and upset if you go away, for example when you leave them at your child-minder or with your baby sitter
9 to 12 months	• seek your attention and cry to get it • become shy around other less familiar faces and be attached to you • feel secure in their close relationship with you and trust that their needs will be met by you • show feelings of happiness by laughing, show feelings of anger by screaming and show feelings of hurt by crying • be able to recognise these ranges of feelings in others, for example, they may get upset easily if they see and hear another small child crying

Milestones for your toddler

Toddler's age:	Your toddler may:
12 to 15 months	• be easily frightened and cry if they are startled by a sound such as a door banging • look for your attention and approval but not always do what you say • have developed a safe and secure relationship with you • react to changes in their daily routine • be able to soothe and comfort themselves, for example, by sucking their thumb, as well as sometimes needing comfort from you
15 to 18 months	• enjoy and thrive on getting your personal attention and praise • get upset when they do not get something they want • be unwilling to share toys with other children
18 to 24 months	• like to have their own way by testing the limits • have tantrums when they do not get their own way • become less frightened than they were of things such as heights or people who they do not really know • learn to deal with short separations from you • not want to go to bed at bedtime • not like it if you are cross with them and they may cry • show resentment of any attention you give to other small children • develop a sense of themselves such as recognising their own face in a mirror

Tips to help your baby to feel safe and secure

- Respond to your baby when they are unsettled or crying – this isn't 'spoiling' them and helps them to become calm.
- Cuddle, touch, sing and talk to your baby.
- Smile at your baby as you hold them close to you.
- Take time to make eye contact with your baby – for example, when you are feeding them.

Tips for encouraging your child's emotional development

Show them affection

Show your child that you love them by giving them lots of physical affection, plenty of cuddles and kisses.

Tell your child that you love them.

Give them time

Make time to play, chat and listen to your child – this lets them know that they are important.

Toddlers need to play on their own and with others – they will learn many life skills such as winning and losing, having fun and chatting to others.

Build their confidence and self-esteem

Talk about your child in a positive way.

Allow them, where possible, to make choices and decisions. For example: "Do you want to wear your blue coat or your yellow coat?" This can help avoid arguments and helps develop their independence.

Encourage them to be as independent as possible, for example by learning to dress or feeding themselves.

> ### Respect your child
>
> All children deserve to be treated with courtesy and dignity, just like adults – your child learns respect from what you do.
>
> For example, suppose you correct your toddler for misbehaviour. Later, you find out that you were wrong. You can show them the appropriate way to behave by saying that you were wrong and you are sorry.

Try to understand your child's feelings

We show our emotions in the tone of our voices and the looks on our faces.

You can help your child understand their feelings and show yours by smiling back at your child when they smile at you. Or put on a sad face and speak to them in a sad tone of voice while you wash and bandage their sore finger. This shows them you feel for them and want to help and comfort them.

Guiding your child's behaviour

As a parent, you want to able to teach your child about the types of behaviour that are acceptable for their age. Encourage positive behaviour by setting clear rules and boundaries. Give your child lots of positive attention when they behave well.

Be consistent

Children thrive in a loving, low-conflict, safe and predictable environment. Give your child the opportunity to be more independent and to make decisions for themselves. Although they may make mistakes, this is part of learning.

By encouraging positive behaviours you are supporting your child to:

- be confident
- get on well with their family and other children
- learn new skills and behaviours
- become more independent over time, solve problems and be able to do more things for themselves as they grow

The following tips can help:

Notice and praise good behaviour

- Praise good behaviour as soon as you see it. Children will appreciate this attention and repeat the behaviour so that they can get more attention.
- Highlight the specific behaviour you want to see more of. For example: "Thanks for putting your dirty clothes in the basket, I really like the way you put them in the basket." That way they will know what you are praising them for and will be more likely to repeat it.

Have clear rules and boundaries

- They need to be short, easy to understand, fair and apply to all in the home.
- Use positive instead of negative words – for example say "do speak quietly" instead of "don't shout".
- Be consistent so children get to know these rules.

Model good behaviour

- You are your child's role model and they are likely to copy what you do – if you act calmly and respectfully it can encourage your child to do the same.

Anticipate problems

- If you know you are going to be waiting somewhere for a period of time, think of activities you and your child can do together to keep them occupied.
- Tantrums are more likely to occur when your child is hungry or tired and having healthy snacks to hand is often a good idea. Try not to plan activities during nap-time or close to bedtime.

Keep to a routine

- Children feel secure if things happen at roughly the same time each day. If you need to change anything, explain why.

If your toddler misbehaves

It is normal for toddlers to test boundaries and limits. It is important to think ahead to how you will manage this behaviour when it happens.

Stay as calm as you can and try not to get upset or angry. Remember that this is all part of your child's normal growth and development.

They are learning from your reaction to their misbehaviour. There are different ways of dealing with this. Here are some options that might work for you and your child.

Consider doing nothing

You could ignore the misbehaviour if it is minor, once your toddler or others are not being put at risk. Toddlers love attention. Generally if they don't get attention when they do something, they will stop.

Taking action

However, you may need to act if the misbehaviour is more serious. This is particularly important if you feel it could cause harm to themselves or others. It is important to let your toddler know that certain behaviours are unacceptable and that you will take action.

Remove the child

You could remove your toddler from where they are misbehaving, explain that this behaviour is not acceptable and why it is not acceptable. Only allow your toddler to return to the activity when they have calmed down.

Change the game

If children are fighting over a toy or activity, you can remove that toy or activity for a short period of time. Explain that you expect them to play nicely and you will return the toy or allow them back to the activity when they calm down.

When you return the toy or to the activity explain the rules again. If the fighting happens again, take away the toy or activity for a longer period.

Follow through

You will need to act quickly, have a plan in place and be consistent. If you don't follow through with what you said your child quickly learns this. They will be less likely to stop the misbehaviour.

Make it clear that the misbehaviour is wrong and not your child, as this may affect their self-esteem. For example, instead of saying "you are a naughty boy, why can't you be good?" you could say "James, pushing Andrea is not nice. It can hurt." Encourage your toddler to wait for their turn.

Have a plan

Plan ahead. It is always best to deal with issues, like tiredness or hunger that might cause your child to be upset or misbehave. For example, if shopping time is clashing with naptime, wait until after naptime to go shopping. If you go shopping with a child who is tired, they are more likely to have a tantrum.

Tantrums

Tantrums are very common and tend to begin around the age of 15 months. A tantrum is sometimes your growing child's only way of expressing their big feelings.

During a tantrum

During a tantrum, your child may do things like shout, scream, kick, bite, throw themselves to the floor or throw things about. Tantrums tend to become less frequent by the time your child reaches the age of 3.

Tantrums can help

Believe it or not tantrums can be a positive thing. They are an opportunity to teach your child how to manage frustration and anger. Being able to deal with challenges and with big feelings like anger and to express them in appropriate ways are really important life skills.

Try to stay calm

Not all children have tantrums, and for some they may only occur occasionally. For other children tantrums are more frequent.

It can be stressful for parents to see their child having a tantrum. Being in public adds an extra element of stress. You may feel embarrassed when your child has a tantrum in public.

When you feel embarrassed, it is harder to remain calm. There are some things you can do to help you to deal with tantrums when they happen.

Managing tantrums

It can be very difficult to stay calm when your child is having a tantrum. You may not realise it, but even when they are having a tantrum your child is watching you to see how you react.

When you stay calm, you are modelling the behaviour you would like them to copy. Your calmness will help your child to feel safe.

Think about why the tantrum is happening

By having a tantrum your toddler is expressing what they are feeling. Perhaps they are hungry or tired. Perhaps they do not want to share a toy with another child. Perhaps they are feeling jealous.

Understanding why the tantrum is happening can help you to deal with it. After all, we all feel angry and frustrated at times, we just express it differently.

Prevention

You can sometimes help prevent tantrums by avoiding your child becoming too hungry or tired. Keep shopping trips short.

> ### Saying "no"
>
> When you say "no", say it firmly and calmly and offer your child another option. For example, encourage other good aspects of their behaviour, such as getting them to join in play with you and others. Remember, it is the tone of your voice and their understanding of the word "no" that is important to learn at an early age.

Be consistent

Don't change your mind just because your child is having a tantrum. If the tantrum has happened because you have said "no" to something, do not say "yes" no matter how tempted you may be.

This might resolve this tantrum, but soon your toddler will realise that tantrums result in them getting what they want.

Wait it out

Sometimes there is nothing you can do other than wait for the tantrum to pass. This can feel like a very long time, especially in public.

Try not to feel embarrassed. Ignore other people who may be around, and focus on remaining calm. People with small children themselves are likely to be very sympathetic, it could be their child next!

Keep your child close

If possible hug and reassure your child, talk out what you think may be going on in their head. For example: "I know you're angry that you can't have sweets..."

Some children will not want to be hugged or touched during a tantrum. Stay with your child to make sure they do not come to physical harm.

Don't try to reason with your child until they calm down

Your young child is too upset to listen to or understand what you are saying. They won't be open to logic.

Look after yourself

If you find yourself becoming angry or upset with your child's behaviour, see if you can get another adult to take over minding them while you take some time out.

Biting, hitting, kicking and other unacceptable behaviours

Most young children occasionally bite, hit and kick others. This might include other children or even a parent. It is normal for young children to test limits.

Strong feelings

These behaviours can happen because your child needs to express a strong feeling such as anger. It may also be their way of telling you they need more personal space.

Sometimes they are simply experimenting to see what will happen or what kind of a reaction they will get. Sometimes biting can happen if your child is teething and in pain.

Teach them it's not okay

As your child grows older, they should learn that these behaviours will hurt others. It is important that you teach your child that these behaviours are not acceptable.

With time, you will notice when these behaviours are more likely to occur and you may be able to prevent them from happening.

Ways to prevent unacceptable behaviours

- Keep an eye on your child, especially when they are around other children.
- Think about when these behaviours normally happen.
- Distract your child with an interesting book or toy if you see them about to bite, hit or kick.
- Provide your child with something they can chew on if you think they are in pain from teething.
- If you think your child bites, hits or kicks when they need personal space, keep an eye on the space around your child. For example: "Jake would you mind sitting over here so Anna has a bit of space?"
- Suggest ways to share and take turns – one idea is to use an egg timer so children can see how long they have to play with the toy before sharing.

How to deal with unacceptable behaviours

Be aware of your own feelings. Count to 10 or take a few deep breaths before you respond. If an older child is hitting their newborn baby brother or sister, it is normal for your protective instincts to make you want to react with anger. Try and react calmly and gently.

Firmly but calmly state that the behaviour is wrong, for example: "No biting. Biting hurts. Look Jake is crying now." Keep it short and simple. It is important to not give too much attention to the behaviour.

Focus your attention on the child who has been hurt by showing concern and sympathy. By doing this, you are not giving attention to the child who has bitten, hit or kicked. Children love attention so by not giving them that attention you make the unacceptable behaviour seem unrewarding. It also shows empathy for the child who has been hurt.

If the other child tries to join in as you soothe the child who has been hurt, remind them to wait because their behaviour was unacceptable.

Learning new skills takes time. You may have to respond consistently like this a number of times. Eventually your child will learn different ways of expressing themselves.

Don't make children play again together unless they want to. It can help to think about activities that don't require sharing, like sand and water play. These may give the children a chance to relax.

Separation anxiety

From about seven months to the age of three, children can be clingy and can cry when separated from you. This is called separation anxiety.

Nearly all children experience separation anxiety at some stage. For some it may last longer than others. Separation anxiety does not happen because you have "spoiled" your baby. It is a normal part of your child's development.

A sign of attachment

Separation anxiety is a sign that your child knows how important you are to them. It shows that they have a strong attachment to you.

Your baby is also beginning to realise that they can communicate their needs and get a reaction. But they do not yet fully understand that when you leave them you will come back.

Helping your child to cope

Separation anxiety can be very upsetting for parents. But you can help your child to understand and cope with their feelings. With your help, your child will learn that they will be okay and that you will return.

Leaving your child with another caregiver is not going to damage them. It actually teaches them how to cope without you. This helps them to become more independent.

How to manage separation anxiety

Remember this will pass. Separation anxiety is completely normal. As your child gets older, they learn that you exist even when you are out of sight.

Until that happens, don't let their separation anxiety stop them from having new experiences or spending time with friends. Don't let it stop you doing the things you need to do, like going to work or going shopping.

- Start with short separations in your own home.
- Leave your child with familiar people.
- If you are arranging new childcare, arrange a few visits to give your child the chance to get to know them while with you. Gradually build up the time your child spends with the new childcare providers.
- Let your child know what you will do together later as this gives them something to look forward to. For example: "When I come back we are going to visit nanny's house."
- Leave something comforting with your child like a favourite toy.
- Make saying goodbye a positive time – smile and say goodbye in a confident and happy way. Don't let your child see that you are sad or worried.
- Never sneak away without saying goodbye. Saying goodbye teaches your child that when you leave, you will return.

Know when to get help. Talk to your GP or public health nurse if your child:

- remains upset for a long time after you leave
- is very distressed
- has separation anxiety going on for a few weeks

Development of your child's sexuality

When you hear the word "sexuality", you may think about sexual activity and contact. However, it is about much more than this. It is about how we develop physically and emotionally, how we express ourselves and how we form relationships with others.

Positive messages

The messages that children get from birth about the human body and intimacy will influence their future development, so it's important that you consider what you'd like those messages to be.

In early childhood, the way you love and nurture your child physically and emotionally is so important. This nurturing care will help your child to love and accept themselves.

Connection

Children learn how to form healthy and connected relationships with those around them. These positive experiences will help them develop the values and skills necessary for forming supportive relationships throughout their lives.

As soon as your child develops speech and understanding, it is important to start speaking to them in an age-appropriate way about their sexual development. Build on these early discussions as they get older.

Babies and toddlers (from birth to 2 years)

Babies and toddlers learn about relationships, sexuality and growing up through the love and care they get from you and their other care-givers.

Fulfilling your baby's need for food, love and shelter increases their sense of safety. It also provides them with opportunities to safely explore through their senses – touch, sound, taste, sight and smell.

All of this contributes to their healthy social and emotional development.

Milestones for your child

Developmental milestones and behaviours	Some of the things you can do to support your child's development
Your child explores their world through their senses of touch, sound, taste, sight and smell.	• Provide lots of opportunities for your child to explore safely. • Play and talk with your child.
Your child experiences attachment. They know their parents and siblings and make strange with new people.	Teach your child about relationships and love through: • making eye contact with them • smiling at them • cuddling, kissing and hugging them • telling them that you love them and that they are important Try to ensure that your child's carers share your approach and values.
Your child engages in unselfconscious play with their genitals if nappies are off or in the bath. Baby boys may have erections.	Babies often play with their genitals. It is a part of their normal exploration. There is no health reason to discourage them. If you feel you need to, it is best to gently distract rather than pull your child's hands away from their genitals. Name all the body parts including the bum, penis, scrotum and vulva when you bathe your child or change their nappy. This makes it normal to refer to these body parts and will help your child to communicate when older.

Screen time

Screen time is the time your child spends in front of a screen. This includes watching programmes and videos and interacting with apps on tablets, phones or other devices.

Devices like tablets and smartphones can be more interactive than traditional TV watching. There may be more advantages to children using interactive technology, for example, in how they learn to move their fingers and hands when touching a screen. However, we do not know enough yet about any benefits to your young child's learning and development.

Avoid screen time under 18 months

Children learn best from talking or playing with their parents. Screen time is not recommended for children under 18 months.

Screen time could mean that your child is spending less time doing other important activities. These include playing, moving around, being active, resting, sleeping, watching and interacting with those around them.

What's the harm?

Too much screen time could increase your child's risk of:

- sleeping less and having sleep issues
- being overweight or obese
- having poorer language skills
- having poorer cognitive skills, for example, issues with their attention

Evidence also suggests that having a TV on in the background can have negative impacts on your child's development.

6 to 18 months

Try to avoid letting your child under the age of 18 months watch or interact with screens other than for video calls with family and friends.

18 to 24 months

- Set limits on their screen time – make sure they spend less than one hour every day in front of a screen.
- Choose high-quality programmes or apps – visit commonsensemedia. org which helps parents make smart media choices for children from 24 months and older.

- Sit with your child when they are playing a game or watching a programme and talk to them about what they are doing, what they see and how it relates to the world around them.
- Avoid programmes or apps that are very noisy or fast-paced, they are not ideal for younger children and could be too distracting or stimulating.
- Make mealtimes screen-free zones.
- Keep the hour before bedtime a screen-free zone.
- Avoid having screens in children's bedrooms, including TVs.

Although many apps are advertised as educational, there is very little evidence to back up these claims for young children.

How to avoid problems with screen time
- Turn off screens in the background when they are not in use as they can still distract babies when they are resting or playing.
- Turn off devices during family times such as meal times.
- Avoid screens for at least 1 hour before bed time as they can impact on sleep.
- Try not to regularly use screens to calm or distract your child. Using screens like this may mean that your child will find it harder to calm themselves as they get older.

Try a toy or an activity

Screen time can be tempting when you are busy and unable to play with your child. Instead, set them up safely in the same room you are in and give them an appropriate toy or activity to occupy them.

Include the rest of the family

It is important to be aware of your family's screen time in the presence of your baby. This is because screen time might get in the way of time spent in activities which are key to building a relationship with your baby.

These activities include:

- making eye contact with them
- touching and holding them
- interacting with them
- responding to their needs

Children also like to copy what they see others do. If they see you spending a lot of time using a smartphone, they will want to do it too. Use your judgment.

Be mindful of your child's exposure to screen time, and make sure screen time does not get in the way of fun childhood activities.

Playing and learning

Play is a very important part of your child's life. From the moment they are born, they are learning about themselves and the world around them.

Play is how your child's thinking, feeling, doing and learning can develop within a safe and secure relationship with you.

Their favourite playmate

As a parent, you are your child's first and favourite playmate. From the earliest weeks and months, spending time playing with them sends an important message to your baby: you are loved, important and fun to be around.

You can find more information on active play on getirelandactive.ie and makeastart.ie

Stages of play (0 to 2 years)

Stage	How your baby plays	Age most apparent	What can I do to help?
Unoccupied	Random movements with no purpose.	This is the first form of play as a baby.	Keep your baby as unrestricted as possible during awake times. For example, watch them as they move around freely on the floor or play mat.

Stages of play (0 to 2 years) continued

Stage	How your baby plays	Age most apparent	What can I do to help?
Solitary **(playing alone)**	Spends most of their time exploring the world around them through their senses. They touch everything around them, taste everything and babble to hear their own voice.	Up to the age of 2.	Have a variety of toys and safe objects in safe reach for your child to explore and touch.
Onlooker	Watches others playing but doesn't join in.	Up to the age of 2.	Let them observe. This is a vital part of play and learning.
Parallel	Parallel play is when socialising is beginning. Children at this stage play next to each other, but don't interact. While they may not acknowledge each other, they are aware that another child is there and it's the first stage of noticing others.	2 to 3 years	Don't force children to 'play together'.

Types of play

Type of play	Importance	What can I do to help?
Physical play	This type of play provides important opportunities for children to build muscles and bones as well as both fine and gross motor skills. Fine motor skills are small movements, for example picking up small objects and holding a spoon. Gross motor skills are the bigger movements, for example rolling over and sitting up.	Encourage them to move as often as possible. Dance with them, play hopscotch or roll some balls.

Type of play	Importance	What can I do to help?
Social play	By interacting with others in play settings, children learn social rules such as give and take, taking turns, co-operation and sharing. It can also support language development.	Bring your child to the playground or parent and toddler groups. Arrange play dates with friends or relatives. They may not 'play together' but increased opportunities to meet other children will develop important social skills.
Constructive play	Constructive play allows children to: • experiment with objects • find out combinations that work and don't work • learn basic knowledge about stacking, building, drawing, making music and constructing It's important to develop their visual spatial awareness (understanding of distance and recognition of their body in relation to other things) and fine motor skills.	Encourage free use of toys such as building blocks and arts and crafts. Don't rush to 'fix' or show them the 'right way' as it's important your child feels they have worked out the best option. It also gives them a sense of accomplishment once they have finished the task.

Type of play	Importance	What can I do to help?
Fantasy play	Children develop flexible thinking. They learn to create beyond the here and now and stretch their imaginations in a risk-free environment.	Provide lots of 'props', for example a whisk and bowl for a 'baker' or a big 'cardboard box' for 'guarding the treasure.' Dress up costumes – bought or homemade – also spark a child's imagination.
Games with rules	Teaches children about fairness. This will help them to learn how to interact with other children.	Start with games with few and simple 'rules' for example, Simple Simon Says or Duck Duck Goose. Very young children won't have the same level of self-regulation as older children. Accept that 'rules will be broken' but that's not a reason to not play.

How your child learns and develops through play

Children's play changes as they grow. Learning and development happens in many ways as your child grows and expresses how they feel and what they want.

Whether it's rough-and-tumble physical, or quiet-and-reflective, all types of play help develop particular skills.

Your child loves playing with you. This helps them feel accepted and understood. Important brain connections develop as your child plays with you. This sets a strong foundation for learning, developing language and life-long positive mental health.

What your child learns from play

Development area	What your child learns to do
Physical	During their first year, they use their whole body and their five senses to play and learn. As they become more mobile, they stretch and grasp things by using their eye and hand movements together, and balance as they move. This movement includes going up and down, pushing and pulling, moving in and out and playing hide and seek.

Development area	What your child learns to do
Intellectual	They begin to test out their developing skills of thinking, reasoning and memory. For example, they explore a soft toy as they play with it to discover what will happen if they squeeze it, taste it or drop it.
Emotional and behavioural	They express their feelings by laughing, smiling and crying. They use play to express themselves. For example, during 'peek-a-boo' they are interacting with you and learning that you are there even when they cannot see your face. They respond to the warmth of your praise and your cuddles.
Social	They play with you and others, as well as play happily on their own while you are near. Encourage your child to mix with other children by visiting a parent and baby or toddler group.

Learning through the senses

You can help your child to develop, learn and grow by stimulating their senses. Everyday play provides the perfect opportunity to explore themselves, you and the world around them.

If your child has difficulty using one of their senses, such as hearing or sight, their other senses help them continue to learn and develop through play.

How your child's senses develop

Sense	Your child
Sight	Your child learns by: • seeing the different colours of playthings • seeing people or toys as they move about • noticing if things are big or small, long or short and shiny or dull looking **What can you do** Show your baby a variety of toys and safe objects.
Smell	Your baby is able to smell before they are even born. Familiar smells can be a source of comfort to your small baby, particularly smells associated with you. Your child learns by smelling different odours such as their parent's perfume or aftershave, the smell of dinner cooking or the smell of freshly cut grass. **What you can do** As your child gets older, talk to them about different smells and act out the action of smelling.
Sound	Your child learns by: • hearing loud and soft noises – these could include laughter and voices, ringing bells or banging drums • listening to you read to them out loud every day **What you can do** Talk to your child about the sounds you hear together, such as the birds singing or the sound of a car horn.
Taste	Your child learns by: • using their mouth to explore and recognise things such as tasting new foods • making funny faces when they taste sweet or sour things **What you can do** Give your child a variety of foods so they develop their taste buds. Make sure that the toys your child plays with are suitable for their age and developmental age and stage because young children use their mouth to explore. They could choke on an unsuitable toy.

Sense	Your child
Touch	Your child learns by: • touching the smoothness of a plastic toy, the coolness of a mirror or the texture of a carpet • feeling the wind on their face **What you can do** Encourage your child to touch your face, grasp your hair and clutch your finger. Try gently stroking your child. This is soothing and it helps nurture the bond between you and your child.

A guide to playing with your child

My child's age	What to do	How they respond and learn
0 to 3 months	Cuddle, touch, sing and talk to your baby a lot. Smile at your baby as you hold them close to you.	Your baby gets excited when they hear or see you. They respond to your touch and the tone of your voice by cuddling into you. Your baby learns to feel safe and bonds with you.

My child's age	What to do	How they respond and learn
0 to 3 months (continued)	Give time for leg kicking without a nappy on.	Your baby's leg muscles will be stretched and these activities will help develop them.
	Introduce a little 'tummy time' every day (see page 129). Place your baby on their tummy for a short time every day. Always supervise your baby when playing on their tummy. Never let your baby fall asleep on their tummy. Try to do tummy time three to four times a day.	Your baby's head, neck and back muscles will be stretched and these activities will help develop them. It also lets your baby experience feeling to the front of their body.
	When your baby is awake in their cot, they may like to look at a brightly coloured mobile. Avoid strings or cords as these could be a choking, strangulation or suffocation risk. Use Velcro if possible.	Your baby shows interest in the moving toy. They learn by seeing different-coloured things and hearing different noises.
3 to 6 months	Continue 'tummy time' every day for a little longer each time. Place suitable toys or objects just out of reach to encourage reaching and moving. Play on a floor mat with your baby.	Your baby's muscles will be stretched and these activities will help develop them. Your baby learns to move about freely. The contact between you and your baby through play is an important part of your baby's development. Your baby laughs readily when you play together. They learn to attract your attention by making noise or waving their arms and hands excitedly. Your baby can also show anger by screaming and squealing instead of crying.

My child's age	What to do	How they respond and learn
3 to 6 months (continued)	Introduce your baby to household objects or toys of different shapes and textures. Include items that can make noise when your baby touches them – like a rattle. Make sure you use toys and objects suitable for their age and developmental stage. Do not use toys that are too small or sharp, as your baby will put them in their mouth as part of learning through play.	Your baby learns about: • bright colours • different feels • tastes and shapes • objects that make noise
	Gently bounce your baby on your knee.	Your baby enjoys the gentle motion and learns about movement.
	Use bath-time to encourage movement.	Your baby enjoys the feeling of the water splashing as they kick their legs.
6 to 12 months	Give your child a few large blocks and toys with wheels to play with.	Your child likes to pick things up, shake them and listen to the sounds they make, especially when they drop them.
	Show your child their image in a mirror.	Your child likes to touch and kiss their image in the mirror.
	Sit down, talk and read with your child.	This helps your child to understand speech and language. Your child is also soothed when they hear your voice. They are able to tell if you are happy by the way you look at them and speak. Your child loves being close to you on your lap and touching the colourful pictures on the book. They get excited when they see pictures of other babies in books or photos.

My child's age	What to do	How they respond and learn
6 to 12 months (continued)	Sing to your child and move to music.	It helps them to develop speech. They will watch your facial and body movements with interest and try to copy them.
	Spend time holding and cuddling your child. You can do this during daily routines such as nappy changing.	Your child feels secure and bonded to you. They show interest in what you are doing with them. You can see this in their eye contact with you and their smiles and babbling.
	Point to your body parts such as your eyes and ears and say each name out loud.	Listening and watching you point to your eyes and ears helps your child to understand the parts of their body. It also encourages them to mimic your movements.
	Praise your child and give them lots of your attention.	Your child loves to be praised for the things they do and may clap their hands to show their happiness. Praise and love builds their self-esteem and confidence.
	Make different funny faces when you play with your child.	Your child laughs at your funny faces and tries to copy them.

My child's age	What to do	How they respond and learn
12 to 18 months	Hide a toy in front of your child while they are watching you do it.	Your child enjoys the game and will quickly find the hidden toy.
	Gently roll or throw a soft ball towards your child.	Your child tries to copy you by picking up the ball and throwing or rolling it back while they are sitting or standing.
	Introduce different things for your child to play and learn with, such as a cardigan with a large zip to encourage your child to grasp small objects.	Your child may be able to unzip a large zipper using their thumb and index finger to hold the zip.
	Play a game of chase with your child.	Your child loves you to chase after them and will laugh and squeal with pleasure as they move about with you following them.
	Play with blocks that stack on top of one another.	Your child will stack up a few blocks after you show them how to do it a few times.

They learn to use their hands and eyes together to build the blocks. |
| | Allow your child some time to play alone while you are near. | Your child learns to play contentedly on their own for a while, knowing that you are nearby. |
| | Play a game of peek-a-boo with your child. | They will show great enjoyment by giggling and smiling and making eye contact with you. |

My child's age	What to do	How they respond and learn
18 to 24 months	Play football with your child using a soft ball – try a variety of shapes, sizes and weights.	Your child learns to balance on one foot while they try to kick the ball with the other foot.
	Play with a tricycle to help your child's movement.	Your child can sit on a small tricycle and move about by pushing their feet forward on the floor. They cannot use the pedals yet. Many trikes have parent-push bars which are great to encourage getting started as well as getting out and about. Try to hold back from doing all the hard work.
	Divide your child's toys into two different boxes and switch the boxes around each week. Use an old shoebox and tea towel as a bed for your child's teddy or doll.	Your child stays interested in the range of toys in the two different boxes. Your child likes to copy what they see and hear you do with them, such as putting their toy into the bed, fixing the blankets and singing a song to the teddy or doll.

My child's age	What to do	How they respond and learn
18 to 24 months (continued)	Make a game out of doing routine things like washing and drying your child's hands before mealtimes.	Your child likes routines and will recognise that washing hands happens before eating.
	Talk through the activities as you do them to encourage interaction and language development.	They also learn to do things for themselves like drying their hands with a little help from you.
	Sit your child on your lap and read stories to them.	Your child may be able to turn over the page to continue the story you are reading to them.
		If you turn the picture book upside down, they may recognise this and try to turn it upright again.
	Encourage your child to mix with other children of their own age by visiting a parent and toddler group.	At this stage your child plays happily on their own while in the company of other children.
		They are not yet ready to share their toys with other children.

Playing with toys

Your child will love exploring toys and household items. Only use a few toys at a time so your child has time to explore each one. Children love it when you play together.

A variety of toys is important to provide different opportunities to learn. It is normal for children to have a preference for certain toys over others.

Open-ended toys

It is a good idea to choose toys that are 'open-ended'. These are toys that your child can use in lots of different ways. They encourage your child to use their imagination, creativity and problem-solving skills.

Open-ended toys include:

Blocks

Your 4-month-old baby might grab a block and bring it to their mouth. At 10 months, they may bang 2 blocks together. They could build a tower at 18 months, while at age 2 pretend the block is a phone!

Balls

Your child can look at a ball and then begin to hold, roll and throw it. Eventually they will learn to bounce a ball.

Cardboard boxes

Watch to see how your child uses a cardboard box. Will it be a shop counter, a car, a boat, doll house or bed? There are lots of possibilities!

Clothes for dressing-up

With some hand-me-down clothes, bits of fabric and old accessories like hats and bags, your child can role-play and build their imagination. See page 194 for more advice on clothes safety.

Arts and crafts

Paper, stickers, crayons and washable markers give your child the experience of creating in a fun and interactive way.

Everyday household items

Pots, pans, baskets, cardboard tubes, tins and lids make great open-ended toys. Make sure they are safe for your child to use and not too small as they may cause choking.

Toy safety

Make sure your child's toys:

- are appropriate for their age and developmental stage
- are in good condition – throw out broken toys because they can be dangerous
- have the CE mark on either the toy or the packaging – this shows that they meet the required safety standards
- do not have strings as they are a strangulation risk
- are stored away when not in use so that they don't cause trips or falls
- are stored in a place that your children do not need to climb to reach them to avoid risk of falls
- cannot fit through the centre of a toilet roll – anything that does is too small and a choking risk

Batteries and button batteries

- Batteries can choke and injure your child. Make sure all battery compartments on toys and other items are secure and can't be opened by your child.
- Keep button batteries out of your child's reach. They are small circular-shaped batteries found in some toys and musical greeting cards. See page 193.

Suitable toys for your child's age

Here are some ideas for toys and everyday household items that encourage your child's development as they grow.

0 to 6 months

- Hold the toys you want your baby to see close to their face – this will help them learn to focus their eyes.
- Play in front of a mirror with your baby.
- Toys should be safe, clean and chewable – remember your baby will try to put everything into their mouth.
- Try shaking a rattle or waving a brightly coloured toy during tummy time.

6 to 12 months

- Toys with different textures that crinkle or feel rough or smooth.
- Rattles and other toys that make a range of noises and tunes.
- Soft colourful balls and toys to push, roll and catch.
- A soft blanket or activity mat with mirrors for your child to touch and toys that make sounds and move about.
- Colourful books with thick pages and pictures of everyday things like faces, cars, tractors or animals.
- Gentle relaxing music, audio stories or nursery rhymes.
- Music that encourages natural movement.
- Blocks that stack on top of one another or small shapes that fit into a larger box.

12 to 24 months

- Soft footballs.
- Empty toilet rolls or kitchen paper rolls.
- Simple insert puzzles and plastic building blocks.
- Chunky non-toxic crayons and blank pages for your child to draw and scribble on.
- Play dough to let your child mould and create things.
- Music that encourages natural movement.
- Books made of thick cardboard with short stories of one sentence on each page.
- Toys for pretend play such as a plastic tea set or an old hat and shoes for playing dress up.
- Big wheeled toys that move about on the floor and can be pushed or pulled along.
- Household things such as a saucepan to place smaller shapes into and a wooden spoon to bang on it.
- A low-sided box that has some everyday things or treasures such as a lemon, a natural sponge and a soft hairbrush. Make sure the objects in the box are safe before you give them to your child.
- Plastic jugs and a basin for pouring, filling and emptying sand and water.

> You or another adult must watch your child at all the times while they play. You are often the best 'toy' that your child needs to play, learn and have fun with. Setting aside time every day for parent-child play is very important.

Keeping your child safe

The more mobile your child gets, the more adventurous they become. But they have no concept of safety or danger. So while your child is busy exploring, they rely on you make sure that their home is a safe place.

A safe place to play

Children don't see danger

Never underestimate your child's ability and speed. Young children move very quickly. In the blink of an eye they can move from where you last saw them.

> The key to child safety is constant adult supervision. In other words, watch your baby and toddler at all times as children do not understand danger.

The basics of child safety

- Have a well-stocked first aid kit and learn basic first aid skills.
- Childproof your home inside and out.
- Put safety measures in place before your child reaches their next developmental stage and age.
- Install child safety equipment to help keep your child safe.
- Share essential safety information with everyone who takes care of your child. This includes grandparents, relatives and babysitters.
- Lead by example – from the earliest age children learn from what we do, so act safely at all times when with them.
- Talk to your child about safety.

Remember that young children do not understand danger and are not capable of being responsible for their own safety.

First aid

Have a well-stocked first aid kit at home. Store it out of sight and reach of your children. Do not store medicines in the first aid kit. Store them separately in a locked high cupboard.

Your public health nurse will give you a HSE child safety wall chart. It includes some basic first aid steps for common injuries. Learn these steps but get medical attention if in any doubt.

Be prepared

The Irish Red Cross has an app with easy-to-follow tips for more than 20 common first aid scenarios. It also has advice about how to prepare for emergencies, including floods, fires and water safety. See redcross.ie

If you get a chance, complete a first aid course. For information you can contact the Order of Malta, The Irish Red Cross or St John's Ambulance. Your public health nurse may also know of first aid courses being run in your area.

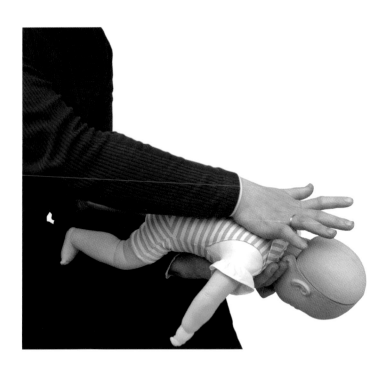

In an emergency

Phone 999 or 112 to contact:

- the ambulance service
- fire service
- Garda Síochána
- the Irish Coast Guard

Know your Eircode

It is a good idea to make a list of easy-to-follow directions to your home and put them in a visible place.

Your Eircode can help an ambulance to find your home. Make a note of your Eircode and put it somewhere obvious in case you or someone else in your home needs to give it to 999 or 112 in an emergency. See eircode.ie

Childproofing your home

Childproofing your home is one of the most valuable actions you can take to help keep your children safe. It helps you spot potential dangers so that you can take action to fix them.

The best way to childproof your home is to:

- Get down on your knees to your child's height.
- Look at every area of your home inside and outside through their eyes.
- Ask yourself: "Is there anything here that could be a danger to my child?"
- Remove the dangers once you have identified them.

Small objects

Remember that babies have a natural tendency to put things into their mouth. Be alert to this when you are childproofing and remove any small objects that could get into your baby's reach.

Checklist

Your public health nurse will give you a child safety checklist. Use this to guide you. Aim to have every box ticked and a plan to fix anything you have not ticked.

Keep updating

Childproofing is not a once-off activity. You need to repeat it regularly as your child becomes more mobile and learns new skills. As your child gets older, you will also need to check for dangers that they can climb to.

Child safety equipment for your home

Safety equipment does not replace the need for adult supervision. However, it can make protecting your child easier.

Equipment you should have

At windows

- Window restrictors that do not need tools for opening on all windows.

Open fires, stoves and heaters (see page 189)

- Sparkguards.
- Fireguards.

In the bathroom

- Non-slip bath mat.
- Toilet locks.
- Bath thermometer.

On furniture

- Brackets or straps to secure TVs and stands, chests of drawers, bookcases and other free-standing furniture to the wall or floor.
- Furniture pads to cover sharp corners on furniture.

In the kitchen

- Fridge and freezer locks.
- Fire blanket.
- Fire extinguisher.

On cupboards

- Cupboard locks.
- Drawer locks.

Alarms

- Smoke alarms.
- Carbon monoxide alarms.

On doors

- Safety door stoppers.

Stairs and steps

- Stairgates at top and bottom of stairs.

First aid and emergency information

- Well stocked first aid kit.
- Basic first aid instructions.
- Emergency contact numbers.
- HSE child safety wall chart.

Other items

- Room thermometer.
- 5-way safety harness on seating devices.

When buying and using equipment

Make sure:

- it meets current safety standards
- is in perfect condition
- you assemble, install and use it correctly – follow the manufacturer's instructions

Preventing common childhood injuries

No child grows up without some bumps and cuts. Most of these are minor, but some can be more serious. Here are some things you can do to try to prevent injuries and accidents.

Did you know?

Most unintentional injuries (accidents) to children under 5 years of age happen in their own home. The good news is that with a little planning you can prevent most of these injuries.

Falls

Raised surfaces

Falls from raised surfaces can cause serious injuries. Never leave your child alone on a baby changer or raised surface.

Don't leave a baby bouncer or any other sitting device on raised surfaces, as your child could topple over.

Stairs

Keep steps and staircases clear. Install stair gates correctly and keep them closed. Use stair gates at top and bottom of stairs. Also use them in areas that pose a trip hazard, like steps at doorways or changes in floor level.

Remove the stair gates once your child is able to climb over them. Show your child how to slowly and safely climb and go down the stairs.

Seats

Only use equipment and sitting devices with a 5-way safety harness — that's a harness with five straps that are all properly secured to provide really effective restraint.

Free-standing furniture

Bookcases, TV stands, chests of drawers, coat stands and other free-standing equipment and furniture can cause serious or fatal injury.

This can happen if the item or its contents falls onto your child. Always secure these items to the wall or floor using brackets or straps.

Make sure items such as kitchen units, dressers, mirrors, fireplaces and mantelpieces are correctly secured to the wall.

TV stands and cabinets

Do not put TVs on cabinets or chests of drawers as children often climb into drawers to reach them.

Always secure TVs, stands and cabinets to the wall or floor with brackets or straps to prevent tip-over incidents.

Windows

Secure all windows with restrictors that do not need tools for opening (so you can escape in case of fire). Where possible, do not place beds, cots, or other furniture near a window. Do not place toy boxes near a window.

Balconies

Make sure your child can't get out onto a balcony without your supervision. Secure balcony doors and fill in any gaps in balcony railings that a child could fit through or use to climb.

Do not place anything children could climb on (like outdoor furniture, plant pots or boxes) near balcony railings.

Floors

Running in socks on a shiny or wooden floor can lead to a nasty fall. Encourage your child to wear well-fitting slippers or go barefoot inside the home.

Other hazards

Make sure:

- walls are finished correctly
- gates are in good working order
- there are no ladders, equipment or items lying around that your child could climb onto

Don't use baby walkers

Baby walkers increase the risk of head injuries, burns, scalds and poisoning.

Stationary activity centres and play pens can provide a safer alternative. These should only be used for short periods and always under supervision.

Children who are not yet walking should spend time on the floor while you supervise. Crawling, shuffling and pulling themselves up supports their motor development.

Motor development is how your child learns to use their muscles to make movements.

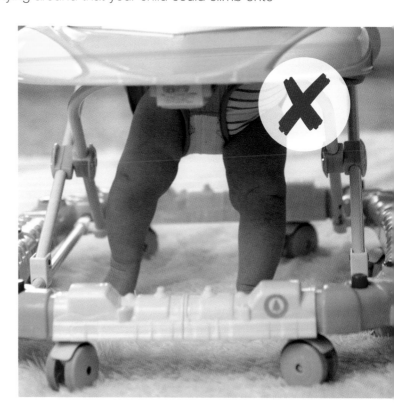

Fire

Smoke alarms

Have working smoke alarms in the hall and landing and aim to have one in every room. Test regularly (once a week is advised) and replace wasted batteries immediately.

Make a fire escape plan and practice it often.

Fireguards and sparkguards

- Use a fireguard and a sparkguard on open fires.
- Stoves and heaters should be protected by a fireguard.
- Fireguards should be secured to a wall.
- Never place anything on a fireguard.

Matches and lighters

Always keep matches and lighters out of your baby's reach. Make your home a smoke-free zone.

Candles

Never leave a lit candle unattended or move it while lit. Position candles away from curtains, draughts and breezes and always out of reach of your child.

Chip pans

Traditional stove-top chip pans are a fire risk. Consider a different method of cooking, for example, using an electrical deep fat fryer.

Sockets

Never overload sockets. Switch off and unplug electrical equipment when not in use.

Burns and scalds

It only takes a tiny amount of hot liquid to cause devastating injuries to babies and young children.

Hot water

Run cold water first, then warm water. Always test bath water with elbow or bath thermometer before putting your child in the bath.

If your bath has a single tap with a hot and cold feed, make sure you run the cold water again to cool the taps so they won't burn your baby.

> The temperature should be about 36°C for newborns. It should be 37°C to 38°C for babies and children.

Never ever leave your child alone in the bath.

See page 88 for more information on bathing your baby.

Hot drinks and foods

Keep hot drinks out of your child's reach or grasp. Hot drinks, even with milk added, are still hot enough to seriously scald your child up to 15 minutes after being poured.

- Never drink or make hot drinks while holding your child and never cook while holding your child.
- Avoid using tablecloths as your child may pull at them.
- Use kettles with a short flex and keep them out of your child's reach.
- Always cook on back rings first, with handle turned in. Use a cooker guard for protection.

Hot bottles and solids

If bottle-feeding, make sure bottle contents are lukewarm and not hot. Check the temperature by shaking the bottle and placing a drop of liquid on the inside of your wrist.

When your child starts eating solids, test food temperature before serving. See page 59 for more information on weaning.

Did you know?

Hair straighteners can reach 200°C and higher – hot enough to fry an egg. They take up to 40 minutes to cool down. Most injuries happen after you have used the straighteners.

It is important to switch them off and unplug them straight away after use. Store them immediately in a heat-resistant bag and out of reach of children.

Choking

Children under 3 are at the highest risk of choking because of the small size of their respiratory tract (airways).

Keep small and unsuitable items out of reach. Be aware that older children may try to share unsuitable objects or food with younger children.

Food preparation

Make sure that food consistency is suitable for your baby's age and developmental stage. Always cut up food to a size that your child can chew and eat safely. For example:

- Cut grapes, cherry tomatoes and similar food into quarters lengthways or smaller.
- Carrot, apple and celery can be cooked until soft or else finely grated.
- Remove or peel skins from sausages or hotdogs and cut lengthways into small pieces (at least as small as your child's small fingernail).
- Use thick pastes like nut butter or chocolate spread very sparingly and spread evenly and thinly onto bread.

- Do not give any child under 5 years of age popcorn, marshmallows, boiled (hard) sweets, chewing gum or nuts.

Eating

Children are more likely to choke if they are moving around while eating. Make sure your child sits in a high chair or at the table and is always closely supervised by an adult. This also gives lots of opportunities for time to talk with your child.

Food choking risks

Bottles

If bottle-feeding, always hold your baby in your arms and hold the bottle in your hand. Never prop or lean the bottle against a pillow or another support – this can cause your baby to choke.

Toys

Use the right toy for your child's age and developmental stage to reduce the risk of choking on toys or bits of toys. Be mindful of older children sharing unsuitable toys with your child.

Always look for the CE mark on toys or their packaging. This shows that they meet the required safety standards. Throw away broken toys. Watch out for older children sharing unsuitable toys with younger ones. See page 181 for more information on toys.

Balloons

Balloons are not toys. Only adults should inflate them and children should be supervised around them.

Batteries

Keep all remote controls and spare or used batteries in a secure place. Make sure all battery compartments on toys and other items are secure and can't be opened by little hands.

Be extra careful with things that don't have locked battery compartments. These include some musical greeting cards, flameless candles and remote controls.

Beware of button batteries

Button batteries are small circular-shaped batteries. They are found in some toys, musical greeting cards, calculators and small electronic devices.

Your child may not choke after swallowing a button battery. But if undetected it can seriously burn their insides.

If you think your child has swallowed one, go to hospital immediately.

Foreign bodies

Your child could get an item stuck in their eyes, ears and nose. Signs may include:

- redness
- irritation
- pain
- bleeding
- discharge
- foul odour

Never try to remove objects that are stuck in your child's ears, eyes or nose as this could cause them serious injury. Always seek medical advice from your GP or the nearest hospital emergency department that treats children.

An object stuck in the nose could cause breathing difficulties or choking if it is breathed in. If your child begins to experience breathing difficulties, go to your nearest emergency department.

Common choking items

Strangulation

Strangulation is most likely to be caused by clothing drawstrings, ribbons, belts, cot bars, window blinds and curtain cords.

Blinds and curtains

Do not fit blinds or curtains with cords attached.

Replace existing cords with curtain or blind wands. Prevent eye injury by keeping wands out of reach of your baby.

Cord tie-down or tension devices (see picture) pull the cord tight and secure it to the wall or floor. They help prevent strangulation risk from continuous loop cords on vertical blinds.

Clothing and jewellery

Your child is at risk from anything placed on or caught around their neck. Never place any of the following on your baby or toddler:

- hair bands
- jewellery (including amber teething jewellery)
- strings
- cords
- belts
- ribbons
- clips
- ties
- clothes and hats with strings or cords

Always remove your child's bib after feeding. Don't allow your children to play with string, cords, ropes or jewellery.

Wires and flexes

Keep electrical flexes, including phone chargers, out of reach.

Fixtures, fittings and furniture

Beware of the risk of getting trapped or strangled posed by banisters, railings, old cots and other furniture with gaps.

Suffocation

Plastic bags and packaging, including nappy sacks

Plastic material can cling to your child's face and cause suffocation. Store plastic bags, plastic nappy sacks and bags, dry-cleaning and other plastic packaging out of reach of children.

Safe sleep

Always keep your baby's cot clear. Never place pillows, duvets, bumpers, sleep positioners, wedges, bedding rolls, toys or comfort blankets into it.

Use cellular aerated blankets which allow air to circulate. See page 202 for more advice about safe sleep for your baby.

Make sure the mattress in your baby's cot and pram is firm and flat. It must fit correctly with no gaps or spaces between it and the edges of the cot or pram.

Sitting devices

Sleeping in a sitting position can cause your child's head to fall forward. This can make it difficult for them to breathe.

Never use a sitting device (like bouncers, highchairs, buggies, swings and car seats) for your child's routine sleep. If they fall asleep in one, remove them and place on their back to sleep as soon as possible.

Long car journeys

If going on a long car journey with your baby, plan for breaks where you can safely park your car. Then take your baby out of the car seat and place them on their back, either on your lap or in the back seat, while you supervise closely.

Return your baby safely to their car seat before you start driving again.

Slings

When using a sling, baby carrier or baby-wearing coat, make sure your child is upright, their head is supported and they don't get too hot.

If your child falls asleep, remove them as soon as possible and place on their back on a flat surface.

See page 88 for more sling safety information.

Drowning

> Never leave your child alone near, with or in water – not even for a second. Even a tiny amount of water is dangerous.

Drowning can happen in silence, in an instant and in a very small amount of water like a puddle or a basin of water.

Children who survive near-drowning frequently have long-term health effects from brain injury.

Watch your child at all times as children can stray very quickly and crawl, walk or fall into water.

Always make sure your child is within your sight and arm's reach.

Bath-time

Never leave your child alone at bath-time. If you need to leave, bring them with you. Don't ask an older child to supervise instead.

Avoid using bath seats. They are not safety equipment. Drowning is a potential danger as your child could slip out of the seat or tip forward or sideways into the water and become completely covered in the bath water.

Always empty bathwater immediately after use. See page 88 for information on bathing your baby safely.

Ponds and water containers

- Empty mop bucket, basins, paddling pools and other water containers after use.
- Store them safely.
- Use toilet latches.
- Look out for and remove containers that could fill with rain water.
- Use protective covers for garden ponds and fence off open water areas. Toddlers are most at risk near garden ponds.
- Keep front and back doors closed and locked at all times.
- The keys should be out of sight and reach of children, but near the door for fire safety purposes.

Pools

Be very vigilant if your child is near a swimming pool, for example on holiday. Make sure there is a locked gate or door separating your child from the pool. You need to make sure your child is properly supervised. Lifeguards do not replace the need for parental supervision.

Swimming aids

Only use arm bands and other buoyancy aids that have an approved safety standard mark (I.S. EN 13138 and the CE mark). They must fit properly. These aids do not replace the need for constant adult supervision.

Poison

Detergents and cleaning products

- Always keep household products in their original child-resistant containers. Be aware that child-resistant containers are not child-proof.
- Store chemicals, household cleaning and laundry products, including laundry and dishwater tablets, capsules and pods in high cupboards.
- Use cupboard safety locks.

> Never use water or soft drink bottles to store detergents, cleaning products, garden and DIY products or any other chemicals.

Garden and DIY products

- Keep garden and DIY products in original containers and out of reach, preferably in a locked shed.
- Dispose of old and unused chemicals and products safely.

Plants

- Remove any poisonous plants indoors and outdoors.
- Get advice from your garden centre when buying plants to make sure they are not a danger to your child.

> **E-cigarettes**
>
> Do not leave electronic cigarettes or their refills in reach or sight of children. These products contain nicotine. It is highly toxic when swallowed or inhaled by children.

Alcohol and cigarettes

Lock alcohol and cigarettes away out of sight and reach. Even small amounts of alcohol can be harmful to children. Cigarette butts have enough nicotine in them to be toxic to babies.

Syringes and needles

Keep needles and syringes locked away. Dispose of them safely immediately after use.

Carbon monoxide

Use carbon monoxide alarms (EN 50291 standard) in every room with fuel-burning appliances.

Medicine and supplements

Keep all medicines, iron and vitamin tablets or supplements in their original containers. Lock them in an overhead medicine cabinet or high cupboard.

This includes 'gummy bear'-type supplements given to older children. Iron is very dangerous for young children if taken in a high dose. Don't use the word 'sweets' when talking about medicines or vitamins.

Try to not to take your own medication in front of your children because children love to copy what grown-ups do.

Follow instructions on medicine labels carefully. Return old and unused medicines to your pharmacist.

Handbag items

Handbags can contain items like tablets, chewing gum, hand gel, cosmetics and perfume. Place all handbags out of your baby's reach.

Public Poisons Line

If you think that your child has taken poison, stay calm but act quickly. Contact the Public Poisons Information Helpline by ringing (01) 809 2166. Save this number to your phone.

Your call will be answered by a specialist who will tell you if medical attention is needed. The helpline is open every day from 8am to 10pm. See poisons.ie

Outside of these hours, contact your GP or hospital. In an emergency, call 999 or 112.

Other dangers in the home

Sharp objects

Always keep sharp objects – such as scissors, knives and pen knives – out of your child's reach and sight.

Electrical equipment

At all times keep the doors closed on your dishwasher, washing machine, dryer, fridge and other similar electrical equipment. Use safety locks.

Sun

If your child's skin is exposed to too much sun, it may increase their risk of skin cancer later in life. It can also cause their delicate skin to become sunburnt. This is painful, itchy and very uncomfortable.

Did you know?

Up to 90% of UV rays can pass through light clouds – so you need to take care on cloudy days too.

Windows

Windows in your car, home and office block most UVB rays but UVA rays can penetrate glass. UVA rays can cause sun damage to the skin, leading to ageing and potentially skin cancer.

For car journeys, use clothing and sunscreen that has a high SPF as well as UVA protection to protect your child's skin.

Consider using window shades in your car to shade your child from the sun. Make sure they have no small or detachable parts that a young child could get hold of.

Seek shade

Keep your child out of direct sunlight, especially between 11am to 3pm. Keep babies under 6 months in the shade as much as possible. Use a sunshade on your buggy or pram.

Cover up

Dress your child in loose-fitting, long-sleeved and light protective clothing. These should be made from close-woven fabric that doesn't let sunlight through. Use a wide brim sunhat that protects the face, neck and ears.

Put sunglasses on your baby as soon they can wear them. Make sure they give as close to 100% UV-protection as possible. Wraparound style offers the best protection.

Use sunscreen

- Choose a UVA and UVB sunscreen made for children and babies with at least SPF 30.
- Patch test it on their skin first – try sunscreen for sensitive skin if their skin is irritated.
- For best protection, apply sunscreen at least 20 minutes before going out in the sun.
- Cover all exposed areas especially the face, ears, nose, lips and tops of the feet.

0 to 6 months

Keep your baby as covered up as possible. Apply small amounts of sunscreen to your baby's exposed skin.

6 to 24 months

Apply generous amounts of sunscreen and reapply at least every 2 hours.

Keep hydrated

Make sure your child drinks enough fluids and does not overheat. They cannot adjust to changes in temperature as well as adults. They sweat less, reducing their body's ability to cool down.

Vitamin D

See pages 56 and 69.

Facts about tanning

A tan does not protect skin from burning. A tan is the skin's way of trying to protect itself from further UV damage. Even when a tan fades, skin damage caused by tanning never goes away.

Getting sunburnt in childhood or adolescence can increase the risk of melanoma in later life. This is the most serious form of skin cancer.

Pets

Never leave your baby or young child alone with a dog, cat or any pet. This is very important whether your baby is awake or sleeping and no matter how well you know the animal.

Introduce your baby slowly to your pet. Existing pets, especially dogs, can be very jealous of a new baby.

Keep all food and water bowls, litter trays and pet toys out of your child's reach.

Model safe behaviour and teach your child how to:

- play safely with pets
- avoid dangerous situations
- respond to danger signs
- wash their hands carefully after all contact with pets and other animals

Bites, scratches and wounds

If your child is bitten or scratched, wash the wound immediately and use disinfectant cream or solution. Always contact your GP if you are worried about a wound or if a wound is not healing properly.

Choosing a pet

Choose a pet that suits your family's lifestyle, home and outdoor space. Snakes, turtles, tortoises and lizards are not suitable for homes with children under age 5. They carry a range of germs that could make your baby very ill or even cause death.

Certain breeds of dogs and any dog with behavioural problems require an additional level of care, control and supervision. Consider carefully if such animals are suitable for your family.

Reducing the risk of cot death

Cot death is also called sudden infant death syndrome (SIDS). It is the sudden and unexpected death of a seemingly healthy baby during sleep.

Cot death does not happen only in a cot – it can happen anywhere a baby is sleeping.

Research has shown that you can take steps to reduce the risk of cot death. Share these key points with everyone who looks after your baby:

Put your baby on their back to sleep

Always place your baby on their back to sleep. This is the same during the day and during the night. Babies who sleep on their tummies have a higher risk of cot death.

Putting your baby to sleep on their back does not increase the risk of choking or vomiting. But placing your baby to sleep on their tummy or on their side does. This is because any vomit will pool at the opening of the trachea (windpipe), making it easier for them to choke.

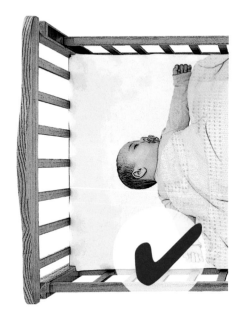

Make sure everyone who looks after your baby puts them to sleep on their back.

Let your baby have some time on their tummy, when they are awake and while you supervise. It is important to begin tummy time from birth. See page 129.

A smoke-free zone

Create a smoke-free zone for your baby. Do not smoke during pregnancy. Don't let anyone smoke in your home, car or around your baby.

A safe sleep environment

For the first 6 months, the safest place for your baby to sleep is on their back in a cot, crib or Moses basket in the same room as you.

Bed sharing or co-sleeping in the same bed can be dangerous. It can increase your baby's risk of suffocation and overheating.

Do not share a bed with your baby if you or your partner:

- are smokers
- have taken alcohol, drugs (legal or illegal) or medication that may make you drowsy
- are over tired

Bed-sharing is not recommended if your baby:

- is less than 3 months old
- was premature (born before 37 weeks)
- had a low birth weight – less than 2.5kg (kilograms) or 5.5lbs (pounds)

Face up and face-free

Keep your baby's face and head uncovered while asleep. This means no hats, hair bands, clothes or covers near their face.

Hair bands can slip over your baby's face and cause suffocation.

Keep covers tucked under your baby's shoulders.

Feet to the foot of the cot

Place your baby with their feet to the foot of the cot.

Keep the cot clear

Keep the cot free of soft objects and anything loose or fluffy that could smother your child. These include:

✗ pillows and cushions	✗ toys	✗ wedges
✗ duvets	✗ bumpers	✗ bedding rolls

Do not use sleep positioners and similar products

They are not necessary and are a suffocation risk. Sleep positioners and similar products do not prevent plagiocephaly (flat head syndrome) or cot death.

A cot in good condition

Make sure the cot is in good condition and properly assembled. The mattress should be clean, firm, flat with no tears and fit the cot correctly.

Make sure your baby does not get too hot when asleep

The room should be between 16°C to 20°C. Don't use too many covers or clothes. It is normal for your baby's hands and feet to feel cool.

Your baby should not wear a hat when being put down to sleep. Babies lose heat through their head. If you cover your baby's head, they may become overheated.

Hats

Your baby should not go to sleep wearing a hat unless you are advised to do so by your doctor or midwife.

Hats are used to keep a baby's temperature stable immediately after birth. They are not needed for sleep after that.

Soothers and dummies

Giving your baby a soother when they are being put down to sleep may reduce the risk of cot death. Wait until breastfeeding is well-established before introducing a soother (see page 35).

Never force a soother if your baby does not like it.

Offer your baby their soother every time they are going to sleep. Do not attach clips, strings, ribbons or chains to soothers. These are a choking and strangulation risk.

Breastfeeding

Breastfeed your baby, if possible. Breastfeeding reduces the risk of cot death, so aim to breastfeed for as long as you can. If feeding in bed, always remember to return your baby to their own cot for sleep.

Sitting devices

Car seats, swings, infant seats, slings, carriers and similar sitting devices are not recommended for routine sleep in the home.

Sleeping in a sitting position can cause your baby's head to fall forward and make it difficult for them to breathe.

If your baby falls asleep in a sitting device, they should be placed on their back to sleep as soon as is possible.

Never leave your baby unsupervised while in a sitting device, whether in the car, home or elsewhere.

Get medical advice early and quickly if:

- your baby seems unwell
- you find it hard to tell if the illness is something minor or more serious

See page 105 for advice on when to contact your GP or get an ambulance. If it's an emergency, dial 999 or 112.

Cot death is still quite rare. While it is important to take all the necessary precautions, do not let fear spoil precious times with your baby.

The safe sleep advice above is intended for babies under 12 months who are well. For babies with specific health needs, extra advice may be given by your healthcare professional.

Car seats

By law, all children under 150cms and 36kgs must use a car seat appropriate to their height and weight. Child car seats must conform to EU standards. Never use a second-hand car seat unless you are sure of its safety history.

In Ireland, 4 out of 5 car seats are not properly fitted, which can lead to serious injury or even death in a crash. Get expert help when fitting your car seat. The Road Safety Authority offers a free 'check it fits' service – see rsa.ie

Make sure your child is secured in a properly-fitted car seat for every journey, no matter how short.

Rearward facing

Keep your child rearward facing for as long as possible. This offers greater protection to their head, neck and spine.

Rearward-facing baby seats are suitable for babies weighing less than 13kg. Extended rearward seats are suitable for children weighing 9 to 25kg. See rsa.ie for more information.

Do not use the front seat if possible

It is safer for children to travel in the back seat in their appropriate child car seat.

Never place your child in a rearward facing car seat in the front passenger seat where there is an active frontal air bag. It is very dangerous and also illegal.

The RSA advises: "Think carefully about driving with a child in the front seat – even in the forward position. You must make sure that the passenger seat is rolled back as far away from the dashboard as possible".

Clothing and the harness

Your child's clothing can affect how the child seat harness fits. Use blankets instead of bulky jackets in cooler weather. This makes sure the harness is making contact with your child's body.

The harness should be tight enough so only two of your fingers can fit between the top of your child's shoulders and the harness straps. Your fingers should be unable to rotate (turn) in that position. Check this before every journey.

Never leave your child in a parked car

Never leave your child alone in a parked car, not even for a short time. Always remove your car keys from your car and keep your car locked. Keep your keys out of sight and reach of children.

Outdoors

Never allow your child access to the road or pathways beyond your home without adult supervision.

Keep outside gates closed and locked. Make sure there are no gaps in the fences or wall surrounding your home. Remove objects near gates and walls that children could climb onto.

Driveways

Due to their small size, children are at risk from reversing vehicles as drivers may not see them. When vehicles are coming into or leaving your driveway, make sure your children are safely inside your home, or an adult is holding them securely in their arms or by the hand.

External doors

Keep all external doors locked. The keys should be out of sight and reach of children but near the door in case of a fire.

Lawnmowers and strimmers

Keep children away from lawnmowers, strimmers and other garden machinery. Don't try to mow the grass and supervise your child at the same time. Ask another adult to supervise your child away from where you are working.

Ladders and equipment

Make sure:

- there are no ladders, equipment or items lying around that your child could climb onto
- walls are finished correctly
- gates are in good working order

Play equipment

Play time is very important and play equipment can help make it fun and exciting. To help keep your child safe:

Safe clothing

Make sure they don't wear jewellery or clothing with ties, strings or cords that could get caught in play equipment.

Equipment safety

Check the equipment:

- is suitable for your child's age and developmental stage
- has a recognised safety symbol such as the CE mark
- is in good condition and secured to the ground
- has no sharp edges or bits sticking out - both at home and in playground

Installing equipment

Make sure you:

- properly assemble play equipment
- place it away from walls, trees, tree houses or hard surfaces, or near places where children might try to jump on or off
- assemble all play equipment according to manufacturer's instructions
- install all safety features

Trampolines

Make sure:

- trampolines have safety padding and safety nets
- children under 6 are not allowed on a trampoline
- only one person is on a trampoline at a time

Child safety on the farm

Working farms have many hidden dangers and children can stray very quickly. Never allow your child to play on the farm. Children are at high risk on the farm from vehicles, machinery, drowning, falls and animals.

Teach your child that the farm is a workplace and dangerous. Be very vigilant also when children visit the farm.

Fenced-off play area

It is not possible to supervise your child safely and work on the farm at the same time. Provide your child with a safe and fenced-off play area, away from the working farm.

Fencing and gates should have mesh right down to the ground. This is so that children cannot climb over or slip through gates or fences. Make sure the play area is in view of the home and your child is supervised.

Poisons

Keep all pesticides, cleaning fluids, chemicals, veterinary medicines and equipment in their original containers and in a securely locked store. Dispose of old and unused chemicals and farm products safely. Never use soft drinks bottles to store chemicals or medicines.

Poisonous plants

Remove any poisonous plants indoors and outdoors. Get advice when buying plants to make sure they are not a danger to your child.

Public Poisons Line

If you think that your child has been exposed to or taken poison, stay calm but act quickly. Phone the Public Poisons Information Helpline on 01 809 2166. It is open from 8am to 10pm every day. Outside of these hours, contact your GP or hospital. In an emergency, call 999 or 112.

Animals

Keep children at a safe distance from livestock and other animals.

Drowning

Use secure protective covers on barrels, troughs and tanks as appropriate. Store basins and buckets out of reach of children. Empty containers can fill quickly after rainfall.

Fence off ponds and other water areas they might fall into.

Slurry pits
Securely cover or fence all slurry facilities.

Falls

Secure gates and doors. Heavy swinging gates or doors are very dangerous, especially in high winds.

Never leave ladders, replacement gates, fencing or similar objects lying around. Children may be tempted to climb them.

Discourage your child from playing with bales of any description. It is very easy for children to fall from stacked bales, resulting in serious injury. There is also a suffocation risk if they fall between bales or bales roll onto them.

Prevent access to areas where there is potential to climb. For example, hay sheds, lofts, high loads, ladders, walls and gates.

Vehicles

Due to their size, children are at risk from reversing vehicles. When vehicles are in use or nearby, make sure your child is safely inside the home or an adult is holding them securely in their arms or by the hand.

Never allow your child near tractors, farm vehicles or machinery. Never leave running vehicles or equipment unattended. Switch off and remove keys from all vehicles and equipment after use.

Never allow your child to travel in tractors, farm vehicles or on quad bikes.

Visitors

Always make contractors aware of the presence of children.

Lead by example

Lead by example by always acting safely yourself. Teach your child how to stay safe on the farm. But remember that young children do not understand danger and are not capable of being responsible for their own safety.

Legal requirements

The Safety, Health and Welfare at Work Act 2005 requires all farmers to prepare and implement a Safety Statement (farmers with three or fewer employees may instead follow the Code of Practice).

Store guns safely and in keeping with the Firearms (Secure Accommodation) Regulations 2009.

Going back to work

If you work outside the home, you will need to make childcare and possibly breastfeeding arrangements. Returning to work after maternity leave can be difficult. Being organised in advance of your return will help make it easier.

How to choose

Deciding on childcare is a big decision for any parent. It is important to discuss your child's needs with the childcare service provider and to know what service they can provide.

When choosing childcare for your child:

- Consider your child's individual needs.
- List your needs such as your working times.
- Talk to other parents – they may know of good crèches, childminders or nannies in your area.
- Arrange visits when there are children present, so you get a feel for the atmosphere.
- Prepare questions before your visit.
- Trust your instincts – you are the expert on your child.

What to check

When you visit, look at the way staff care for, talk to and listen to children in their care.

Check:

- the staff are qualified and Garda-vetted
- there is enough staff to supervise the children at all times
- the premises is safe and secure
- there are appropriate childcare policies and procedures in place – examples include child protection, behaviour management and accidents
- the fees, hours and holiday periods

References

Always check references before deciding on childcare.

Information and advice

Your city or county childcare committee

Your city or county childcare committee can provide a list of childcare providers in your area. See pobal.ie for contact details.

The Child and Family Agency (Tusla)

On tusla.ie you will find:

- a list of child care services in your area
- tips on choosing a pre-school
- inspection reports for pre-school childcare facilities

Childminding Ireland

You will also find a list of childminders in your area and advice on choosing a childminder at childminding.ie

Barnardos

Barnardos has a guide on what to look for called 'Quality Early Years Care and Education' which you can find on barnardos.ie.

Types of childcare options

Services include:

Full day care such as a crèche

These facilities care for children for more than 5 hours a day.

Sessional services

These services offer a planned programme of up to 3.5 hours per session. These include playschools, naíonraí (Irish language nursery schools or playschools) and Montessori.

Childminders

Childminders care for children in the home. A childminder can care for up to five children under six years of age. This includes the childminder's own children if they have any. Parents and childminders arrange their own terms and conditions.

Affordable childcare

Affordable childcare provides childcare for families on lower incomes, and also supports parents to return to work or education. Contact your local City or County Childcare Committee for information on affordable childcare services in your area. Find your local committee at myccc.ie

See www.ncs.gov.ie and citizensinformation.ie for information on affordable childcare.

Settling your child in

You will be less stressed if you are comfortable with your childcare arrangements and if your child has had the opportunity to settle in with the childminder, crèche or family member.

Several weeks before your return to work date, introduce your child to your childcare provider, and begin the process of "settling in". They will have established routines for getting babies used to their service.

Allow yourself plenty of time to prepare for putting your child in childcare and take time to learn about what you should expect from a childcare service.

Babysitting arrangements

Tips on choosing a babysitter

- Consider a babysitter's level of experience, sense of responsibility and ability to care for your child.

- Meet with other parents in your area to get recommendations and tips on suitable babysitters.

- Find out the local rate for babysitting before you hire someone and discuss pay with your sitter so that you are both comfortable with the payment beforehand.

- You know you have chosen a good babysitter when your child looks forward to seeing them and appears comfortable and relaxed with them.

What to discuss with your babysitter

Chat about your child's night time routine so your babysitter is familiar with it. This includes telling them how often you would like them to check on your sleeping child.

Encourage the babysitter to visit your home and get to know your child. Show your babysitter the layout of your home including:

- where the fire exits and door keys are
- where you keep first aid equipment
- how equipment such as cookers and the heating system works
- safe sleep guidelines – see page 202

Discuss security issues with your babysitter so that they know what to do if someone calls to the door.

Going back to work

Before you leave

Talk to your babysitter about what you expect from them. Let your babysitter know to the nearest half hour when you are due to come home.

Write down the following numbers and give them to your babysitter:

- Your mobile number.
- Emergency telephone numbers such as 999 and Gardaí.
- Your home's Eircode – you can find it on eircode.ie
- The address and telephone number of where you are going.
- Another contact number such as a local family member or friend in case your babysitter cannot contact you in an emergency.

Do not leave a babysitter to cope with an already sick or upset child who will not settle.

Going back to work and breastfeeding

You can continue to breastfeed your baby when you go back to work.

> Before you go back to work, you need to discuss arrangements with your employer. You will need:
>
> - breaks so that you can express breast milk
> - a private place to express breast milk
> - a fridge to store the milk until you take it home
>
> Talk to your public health nurse, a support group or a friend who has returned to work and continued to breastfeed her baby for advice.

If you return to work within 6 months of the birth

In Ireland, by law, breastfeeding employees are entitled to 60 minutes time off or a reduction in work hours in an eight-hour working day without loss of pay for up to 26 weeks (6 months) after birth. This may be taken in the form of one break of 60 minutes, two breaks of 30 minutes or three breaks of 20 minutes.

If you plan to do this, you must let your employer know in writing of your intention to return to work and the date. Write to them at least 4 weeks before your return to work date.

If you return to work after 6 months

Mothers returning to work after the six-month time period do not have a legal entitlement to breastfeeding breaks. However, talk to your employer about breastfeeding, as some workplaces have policies that will support you for as long as you continue to breastfeed.

During the work day, you can express breast milk and save it for your baby.

Your benefits and leave entitlements

There are various state benefits, schemes and leave entitlements for pregnant women and parents.

There may also be extra supports and entitlements. For example, if your child has special needs. See page 141.

The information below was correct at the time of going to print but may change in the future.

The Maternity and Infant Care Scheme

As well as covering your public medical care during pregnancy, the scheme also provides for two free visits to the GP after the birth.

Your GP will examine your baby at 2 weeks and both you and your baby at 6 weeks. See page 6.

Other services

The public health nurse (PHN) visits you and your baby at home free of charge, usually within 72 hours of returning home from hospital.

You and your baby will be offered various free screening programmes such as newborn bloodspot screening (heel prick). See page 6. Your midwife or PHN will arrange this for you.

GP visit card for children under 6

Children under the age of six are entitled to free visits to a participating GP. All children under six who live and intend to live in Ireland for one year are eligible. This card also covers out-of-hours and urgent care.

The GP visit card also covers your child for assessments at ages two and five and care for children with asthma.

If your child has a medical card

If your child already has a medical card, you don't need to register them for the GP visit card.

However, if your family circumstances change and your family is no longer eligible for medical cards, you can then register your child for a GP visit card if they are under the age of six.

Registering for a GP visit card

You will need to register your child for the card. This can be online or by post. See hse.ie for details.

If you have any questions before registering, you can phone lo-call 1890 252 919.

Health service schemes

There are schemes to make the cost of medical and healthcare more affordable.

Some schemes are means-tested. A means test examines all your sources of income. However, some income is not taken into account when your means are calculated. See citizensinformation.ie for information on means-testing.

Other schemes are based on age groups. Some are available to all residents.

Examples include:

- Medical cards.
- The Drugs Payment Scheme.
- European Health Insurance Cards (EHIC).
- GP visit cards.

See hse.ie for more information on these schemes.

Maternity benefit and adoptive benefit

Maternity benefit is a payment to employed and self-employed pregnant women.

Adoptive benefit is a payment to an adopting mother or to a single adoptive father from the date your child is placed with you. It is available to both employed and self-employed people.

For more information, contact:

- Social Welfare Services (maternity benefit section) on lo-call 1890 690 690, lo-call the leaflet request line at 1890 20 23 25 or see welfare.ie
- Citizens Information at your local centre, phone 0761 07 4000 or see citizensinformation.ie
- your employer

Maternity leave

You are entitled to 26 consecutive weeks of maternity leave and 16 weeks additional unpaid leave.

You must tell your employer in writing at least 4 weeks before you start your leave.

Premature babies

If your baby was born prematurely before your maternity leave was due to start, you can apply to extend your maternity leave and maternity benefit.

See welfare.ie for more details.

Adoptive leave

You are entitled to 24 consecutive weeks of adoptive leave if you are an adoptive mother or a single adoptive father in paid employment. You are also entitled to a further 16 weeks unpaid leave after the end of your adoptive leave.

You must inform your employer in writing four weeks before you start your leave.

For more information, talk to your employer or contact Citizens Information at your local centre, phone 0761 07 4000 or see citizensinformation.ie

Paternity leave

You are entitled to two weeks of paternity leave following the birth or adoption of a child if you are the:

- father of the child
- spouse, civil partner or partner living with the mother of the child
- parent of a donor-conceived child
- spouse, civil partner or partner living with the adopting mother or adopting father of the child

You can take paternity leave at any time in the 26 weeks following the birth or adoption. You must tell your employer in writing at least four weeks before you start your leave.

Paternity benefit

Your employer does not have to pay you for paternity leave. You may be eligible for paternity benefit for this time off.

For more information, talk to your employer or contact Citizens Information at your local centre, phone 0761 07 4000 or see citizensinformation.ie

Parental leave

When you return to work, you can take parental leave. Both parents are entitled to take parental leave.

For more information, talk to your employer or contact Citizens Information at your local centre, phone 0761 07 4000 or see citizensinformation.ie

Child benefit

Child benefit was previously known as children's allowance. It is paid to the parents or guardians of children under 16 years of age, or under 18 years of age if the child:

- is in full-time education
- is doing Youthreach training
- has a disability

For the most up-to-date information on the rates, see citizensinformation.ie

Who to contact

- Citizens Information – contact your local centre, phone 0761 07 4000 or see citizensinformation.ie
- Social Welfare Services (child benefit section) – locall 1890 400 400 or see welfare.ie

One-parent family benefit

One-parent family payment (OFP) is a payment for men and women under 66 who are bringing children up without the support of a partner.

To get this payment you must meet certain conditions and do a means test. More information is available from your local Social Welfare Office. Lo-call 1890 500 000 or see welfare.ie

Other benefits you may qualify for include

- Back to work allowance.
- Back to education allowance.
- Disability payment.
- Domiciliary care allowance.
- Exceptional needs payment.
- Working family payment.
- Medical card.
- Rent supplement.
- Housing assistance payment.
- Unemployment payments.
- Back to school clothing and footwear allowance.
- Health and safety benefit.

More information

- Citizens Information – contact your local centre, phone 0761 07 4000 or see citizensinformation.ie
- Your local Social Welfare Office – lo-call 1890 66 22 44 or see welfare.ie

Health or medical expenses

You may also be entitled to tax relief on health or medical expenses. See revenue.ie for information.

Finally

We wish you well with your child. This is such a special time for you and your new family. You are supporting your child to grow up to be healthy, resilient and confident.

Look after yourself

Be kind to yourself, it is important to look after yourself and your relationships.

Don't be afraid to ask questions

Trust your instincts and don't be afraid to ask questions. There is no such thing as a silly question.

There is no training for having a child and you are learning as your child grows as to what works for you and your family.

Your next book

This book is part of a series of three books to support you and your family during the first five years of your child's life.

Your public health nurse will give you the last book in the series, My Child: 2 to 5 years, close to your child's second birthday.

Our website

Go to mychild.ie for more information on your child's health and development, plus advice on parenting.

Enjoy this time

Enjoy your child as they grow and develop, learn to take care of yourself too and prioritise this special time for you and your family.

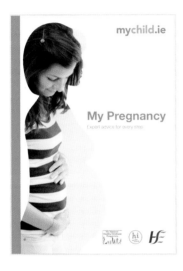
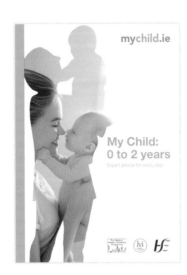

Index

Index

Index